Clinical Psychology

Kevin Brewer

Clinical Psychology

Kevin Brewer

Heinemann Educational Publishers
Halley Court, Jordan Hill, Oxford, OX2 8EJ
a division of Reed Educational & Professional Publishing Ltd

OXFORD MELBOURNE AUCKLAND
JOHANNESBURG BLANTYRE GABORONE
IBADAN PORTSMOUTH (NH) USA CHICAGO

Heinemann is a registered trademark of Reed Educational & Professional Publishing Ltd

Text © Kevin Brewer, 2001

First published in 2001

05 04 03 02 01
10 9 8 7 6 5 4 3 2 1

British Library Cataloguing in Publication Data
A catalogue record for this book is available from the British Library

ISBN 0 435 80660 2

Typeset by Wyvern 21 Ltd, Bristol
Picture research by Elaine Willis
Printed and bound in Great Britain by The Bath Press Ltd, Bath

Acknowledgements
The publishers would like to thank the following for permission to reproduce copyright material: *The Guardian* for the articles on pp. 45, 59, 66 and 68; *The Times Educational Supplement* for the article on p. 5 © Times Supplements Limited.

Cover photograph by AKG London

The publishers would like to thank the following for permission to use photographs: Associated Press, p.39; Austrian Archive/CORBIS, p. 51; Bettmann/CORBIS, pp. 29 and 52; Camera Press, pp. 40 and 56; CORBIS, p. 61; Mitchell Gerber/CORBIS, p. 61; Hulton, p. 16; David Lees/CORBIS, p. 26; Roger Ressmeyer/CORBIS, p.33; Science Photo Library, p. 67.

The publishers have made every effort to contact copyright holders. However, if any material has been incorrectly acknowledged, the publishers would be pleased to correct this at the earliest opportunity.

Tel: 01865 888058 www.heinemann.co.uk

C Contents

1 Introduction

> Within any society there are people who are different to the majority. The questions to answer are 'Why are there such people?' and 'Is it a problem?'. Clinical psychology is concerned with these questions, and particularly with the people who need help. In Western society, such people are seen as being mentally ill. This book is divided into four chapters, with each chapter considering the different issues that are likely to arise within the context of clinical psychology.

Chapter 1

The whole issue of what is normal and abnormal is explored in this chapter. There are a number of definitions, each with its own problems, as well as cultural and sub-cultural differences.

Chapter 2

Within clinical psychology there are a number of different models of what causes mental disorders. In this chapter details of the five most important models are outlined – the medical, psychodynamic, behavioural, cognitive and humanistic models.

Chapter 3

There are many different types of mental illness. This chapter concentrates on anxiety disorders, bipolar disorders, schizophrenia, and eating disorders. The main symptoms and causes of each disorder are discussed.

Chapter 4

The final chapter looks at ways of treating mental disorders. There are many different therapies used, but this chapter concentrates on the main techniques of the five models outlined in Chapter 2.

How to use this book

This book has a number of features to help you understand the topic more easily. It is written to give you a wide range of skills in preparation for any of the new AS and A level psychology syllabi. Below is a list of the features with a brief summary to explain how to use them.

1 Real Life Applications

These consist of 'text boxes' that develop further a concept already discussed within the main text. Often they provide articles or outlines of studies. In all cases they attempt to apply theory to 'real life situations'.

2 Commentary

These paragraphs appear throughout the book. They follow on from issues raised within the main text. They serve a number of functions: to provide an evaluation of the earlier text, to clarify a point or highlight some related issue. Sometimes they provide 'for' and 'against' debates.

3 Key studies

As the title implies these are descriptions of important studies within a specific area. There are two of these for each chapter. They briefly identify the aims, method, results and conclusions of the study. This feature helps you to understand the methodology of research.

4 Questions

Each Real Life Application has two or three short answer questions, which are designed to test a range of skills including summarising, outlining and evaluating. All of these activities are designed to allow you to acquire the 'key skills' outlined within the syllabi. In addition, two or three 'essay style' questions are included at the end of each chapter. They specifically relate to the material covered within that chapter.

5 Advice on answering the questions

There is a short section at the end of this book that gives brief advice on answering all the essay questions. It also provides answers to the short questions presented in this book.

1 Defining normal and abnormal

This chapter looks at what underlies clinical psychology – in other words, the assumption that certain individuals are 'different', 'abnormal', 'mentally disordered' or 'mentally ill'. These terms all say the same thing, but the actual term used depends on which definition is preferred. Altogether, the aim is to establish what is normal behaviour and what is abnormal behaviour. Historically and culturally this has varied, and even today there are no universally agreed definitions.

Real Life Applications that are considered are:

- RLA 1: Eccentricity
- RLA 2: Normal or abnormal?
- RLA 3: Nude horizons
- RLA 4: Worldwide definition of mentally healthy
- RLA 5: What is madness?
- RLA 6: Whose mind is it anyway?

What is normal?

Rosenhan and Seligman (1989) succinctly stated that 'normality is simply the absence of abnormality'. Unfortunately, this definition is not that helpful in practice. Often what is abnormal behaviour is also associated with what is morally unacceptable. Stone (1975, quoted in Gleitman, 1991) shows how the definitions of normal, abnormal and evil can overlap (see Figure 1.1, page 2). Thus abnormal behaviour can require the response of the legal or the medical profession.

Commentary

In Figure 1.1, areas G and F are very difficult because there is a clash between the legal and the medical profession. The term 'insanity', for example, is a legal term used in court to show that the individual does not know what he (or she) is doing at the time of the crime, while 'deviant' is a more common term used for anybody who does not 'fit in'.

Problems with normality

There are a number of points to consider when trying to establish what is normal or abnormal. First, it is a continuum rather than two separate groups (see Figure 1.2, page 2).

Some abnormalities are slight and probably fall within the range of normal variation (area A in Figure 1.2) – for example, the reaction to a snake. Some people are happy to touch snakes and hold them; others do not want to do these things but do not have a problem with snakes.

Extreme cases of abnormality are easier to spot (area D in Figure 1.2) – for example, people who cannot even say the word 'snake' without having a phobic reaction, and would never go anywhere where snakes could be found. But where is the line drawn between normal and abnormal (points B and C in Figure 1.2) – for example, reacting badly to a snake crawling over you or such a reaction to seeing a snake? Here the decision can become arbitrary, rather than any objective means of deciding.

Another problem in defining what is normal or abnormal is that there is no single way to define them because there are no objective facts. It is also assumed that it is possible to divide normal and abnormal behaviour. This is highlighted by the case of 'eccentrics' (see Key Study 1, page 2, and RLA 1, page 2).

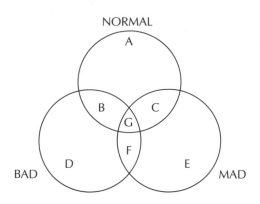

Gleitman, 1991.

Figure 1.1: Overlap between normal, abnormal and evil based on Stone (1975)

Key to Figure 1.1:

A = 'normal': this person behaves appropriately for his (or her) culture in every way.

B = 'troublesome': a person here is predominately normal in his behaviour, but occasionally commits an illegal act, like reckless driving. It is more appropriate for the law to deal with such behaviour.

C = 'self-destructive': this person has a particular behaviour that is causing problems in his/her life (like alcoholism). Here it is appropriate to offer medical help.

D = 'criminal': the person is fully committed to a criminal lifestyle, and is outside the normal realms in this way. There is nothing medically wrong.

E = 'crazy': the person here is mentally ill to such a degree that his whole life is affected. He/she is in need of medical help.

F = 'psychopath': this category is very controversial. An individual here could break the law, but need medical rather than a legal response. If a psychopath kills somebody, he/she is usually sent to a special psychiatric hospital rather than to prison.

G = 'objectionable': the person in this category is different from the psychopath because he/she has some awareness of his/her behaviour ('normal'), which the psychopath does not. But, for example, in the case of child abuse, individuals are breaking the law and seen as mentally ill. Again this is an area of controversy as to how to deal with such behaviour – prison or special hospitals.

Figure 1.2: Normal/abnormal continuum

KEY STUDY 1

Researchers: Weeks and James (1995)

Aim: To study eccentrics for common patterns of behaviour, and also to see if they could be classed as mentally ill.

Method: 100 eccentrics were interviewed in detail.

Results: The researchers drew out 15 common characteristics of eccentrics including non-conformity, creativity, idealism, happily obsessed with a 'hobby horse', intelligent, unusual eating and living habits, and not particularly interested in the company of others. Concerning the question of whether these people were mentally ill, Weeks and James gave a Present State Examination (PSE) using the symptoms typical of schizophrenia, and there was little evidence of serious mental illness (see Table 1.1).

Conclusions: Eccentrics are probably close to the divide between normal and abnormal, and may move back and forth. Importantly, they are usually unconcerned about the views of society upon their behaviour.

	Absent	Partial/ mild	Full/ severe
Delusion of thought being read	62	38	0
Thought insertion	100	0	0
Thought broadcast	94	5	1
Thought block	70	29	1
Delusions of alien forces controlling mind	88	11	1
Auditory hallucinations	70	25	5
Visual hallucinations	65	26	9
Delusional misinterpretation	69	25	6
Delusions of persecution	57	41	2
Religious delusions	55	41	4
Paranormal delusions	70	27	3

Weeks and James, 1995.

Table 1.1: Frequency of Present State Examination (PSE) symptoms of schizophrenia among sample of 100 eccentrics (%)

Real Life Application 1: Eccentricity

John Slater holds the record for being the only person to have ever walked from Land's End to John O'Groats in his bare feet, wearing only his striped pyjamas and accompanied by a dog (which was wearing suede bootees).

Slater has held a number of jobs: Royal Marine bandman, Commando, truck driver, steward on a luxury yacht, social worker, insurance salesman, waiter, painter and decorator, and public speaker. He has lived homeless in London so that he can learn more about himself. At the time of the book, he was living in a cave on the seashore for the last ten years. The cave filled with sea water at every high tide.

Slater has been married three times, and has endless ideas like volunteering to be a human exhibit at London Zoo to raise money to help in the conservation of pandas. His motto is 'Wag your tail at everyone you meet'.

Weeks and James, 1995.

Summary

- John Slater has never had a 'normal' job or life. He has done many things, most of them with idealism. He has attempted many times to raise money for charity.

Questions

1 Is John Slater abnormal because he has not held down a job for a reasonable time?

2 Is he mentally ill?

3 What should be society's response to such an individual?

Defining abnormality

There are a number of definitions and means of classifying abnormal behaviour. They can be grouped as follows.

- Norms: social; statistical.
- Specific measures: maladaptive/unexpected behaviour; highly inconsistent/consistent behaviour; exposure to psychiatric treatment; functional versus dysfunctional behaviour.
- Subjective assessment: personal distress; others' distress; understanding in relation to the self.
- Mental health.
- Mental illness.

Table 1.2 gives an example of these definitions of normality and abnormality as applied to wearing the clothes of the opposite sex. RLA 2 (see page 4) gives other examples of normal and abnormal behaviour.

Criterion	Male	Female
Social norm	Abnormal, unless in play/fancy dress etc	Normal – e.g. trousers today, but abnormal in Victorian times
Statistical norm	Abnormal – minority behaviour	Normal – majority
Maladaptive behaviour	Abnormal	Normal
Mental health	Abnormal	Normal
	But Kinsey *et al* (1966) report societies where seen as possessing magical powers or 'third sex' (e.g. Mohave Indians)	
Medical model	DSM IV* 302.3 'Transvestic Fetishism' – heterosexual male who has 'recurrent intense sexually arousing fantasies, sexual urges, or behaviours involving cross-dressing'	No equivalent category

* DSM IV is the current classification system used by psychiatrists in America (see Chapter 2, page 16).

Table 1.2: Wearing the clothes of the opposite sex – abnormal behaviour?

Real Life Application 2:

Normal or abnormal?

1 Mary is a teenager who rarely eats, except on 'feast days'. On these days, she will go to the supermarket early in the morning and buy enough food to eat for the rest of the day. This is followed by a period of vomiting. 'Feast days' happen two or three times a month.

2 Diane is a housewife who finds every day very difficult to survive while her husband is working long hours. She overcomes this by spending the day shopping and building up debts on her credit cards.

3 Bob lost his job, then his marriage broke down. He is now first in the pub when it opens at lunch time and the last to leave at closing time in the evening. Each day he seems to be drinking more. Often he cannot remember the day before.

4 Amy is fourteen years old and pregnant. She refuses to name the father of the child.

5 Alan is a successful businessman. In the evenings, when by himself, he prefers to walk around the house in women's clothes. He finds this very relaxing and an escape from the demands of his business life.

6 Barry is a collector of newspapers. He spends most of his days looking for discarded newspapers, which he takes home. His home is completely filled with old rotting newspapers. When asked why he does it, he says that it is his calling.

Questions

1 In each of the above cases, is the individual normal or abnormal? Give reasons for your answers.

Deviation from the norm

This approach to defining normal or abnormal behaviour has predominated historically and still has influence today. It is based on the concept of norms.

These are beliefs about what is normal behaviour, and that anybody who does not show them is abnormal. The norms may be social-based or statistical.

Commentary

'A norm is a rule, standard, or pattern for action (from the Latin norma, a carpenter's square or rule)' (Williams, 1968). An alternative term is 'customs', which are seen as obligatory.

There are two types of social norm. The first type are known as descriptive norms, and they are the common behaviours that most people have. These norms tell us what is 'correct' conduct for a particular situation. In the main, it is about following the lead of the crowd – that is, conforming.

The second type are called injunctive norms. These are the shared expectations within a society, culture or group regarding what is acceptable/unacceptable behaviour. The first set of norms are called the norms of 'is', while the second set are the norms of 'ought'.

Social norms

Society establishes what is normal based on its values and beliefs. Gorenstein (1984) summarizes this as 'behaviour that is beyond the bounds of social acceptability would be considered a manifestation of mental illness by this definition'. Thus the concept of 'social acceptability' plays an important part in this definition. Under this definition, there would be different norms for different behaviours as well as a continuum of acceptability (see Figure 1.3, below).

Social norms will thus tend to vary at different times throughout history. For example, Petkova (1995) argues that naming women as witches in the Middle Ages was a means of controlling those women who committed unacceptable behaviour for that society, and had nothing to do with witchcraft.

Norms about behaviour develop in any group or social situation, and the group/society automatically works to maintain the norms, like putting conformity pressures on deviants. Schachter (1951) set up a small discussion group with students that contained three 'stooges' (individuals working with the experimenter who appear to be ordinary participants). One of the stooges was the 'mode person', always

Desirable/ obligatory	Mildly unacceptable	Moderately	Very
e.g. use cutlery	e.g. poor manners	e.g. excessive gambling	e.g. murder
Response	e.g. staring/ridicule	e.g. private rejection	e.g. imprisonment

Figure 1.3: Continuum of acceptability

agreeing with the group, one was the 'slider', who started by disagreeing then came to conform, and the final 'deviant' was always disagreeing with the group. Schachter was interested in how the group would treat the 'deviant'. At first, the 'deviant' was given attention, but when the person did not conform, they were ignored. The 'slider' was given attention throughout because they responded to the pressure to conform.

However, there are many reasons why this definition is unsatisfactory. Most important, it is subjective – that is, it is based on the opinion of certain groups. In practice, the norms of society are based on those of the élites (including the government), and what they want becomes the norm. For example, in the Soviet Union after the Second World War, political dissent was defined as abnormal behaviour. Thus, in a totalitarian society, individuals calling for democracy were classed as mentally ill and put into psychiatric hospitals.

In practice these hospitals and the terms of mental illness were means of controlling those who did not do what the government wanted. What develops from this situation is that those seen as abnormal are labelled and discriminated against. Van der Berg (1955) talks of a 'vocabulary of denigration'.

Technical terms like 'schizophrenia' become insults, suggesting that there is something wrong with the person causing them to be like that. Furthermore, abnormality is often confused with illegality.

In practice, there are different types of deviancy, as outlined below:

- Individuals who do good with the deviancy – for example, suffragette campaigners defied the norms for women of late nineteenth- and early twentieth-century society, which led to electoral rights for women.
- Individuals who do bad with their deviancy.
- 'Harmless deviants': individuals who do not fit into the norms but who are not harming anybody – for example, naturism (see RLA 3). Often, these individuals are criticized by society for no reason except that they do not fit into the social norms.

Real Life Application 3:
Nude horizons

In Britain there are around 25 000 'committed naturists', and their interest dates from the 1920s with the formation of the Sunbathing Society and the New Gymnosophy Society. The modern day organization is known as the Central Council for British Naturism. Richard Daniels is the president: 'What most people don't understand is that naturism is not at all sexual. It is simply to do with feeling comfortable and relaxed about your body. We're much less judgmental about shapes, sizes and oddities.'

Another misconception is that people join the naturist clubs for the 'wrong reasons'. Daniels remembers only one case in many years of a man who kept peeping out from behind his newspaper and ogling people. He was quickly asked to leave.

What about the effects of bringing up children in the naturist tradition? Daniels has three grown-up children who show no apparent ill-effects. Teachers have also been worried about being naturist and what parents would think of them. For example, Anne Summerhill was reported in the local newspaper, and the parents signed a petition for her dismissal. However the controversy blew over. Anne is unhappy because many parents saw her as immoral, even a 'swinger'.

Naturists argue that without clothes everybody is equal, which is different to how 'textiles' (non-naturists) respond to people's clothes.

Adapted from 'Nude Horizons' by Nicki Household, *The Times Educational Supplement*, 25 June 1999 © Times Supplements Limited.

Summary

- Naturism is a desire to be without clothes and has a small number of supporters in this country. Often the motives of naturists are seen as sexual or 'unhealthy' by non-naturists.

Commentary

The whole approach of a social norm assumes that the norms are always right or desirable. In Nazi Germany norms were established by the government that encouraged hatred and mistreatment of Jews, Romany people and those with disabilities. In particular, these groups had to wear distinctive clothing and the norm for Germans was to spit at them. The reason these groups were classed as abnormal was because they were not white Aryan Germans. The use of social norms is open to moral and ethical abuse.

In USA between the two world wars, in some states it became acceptable to sterilize women who were classed as 'feeble-minded' (low intelligence).

Criticisms of social norms

Conversely, there may be individuals who conform but who are suffering from a problem – for example, 'conforming neurotics'. Part of the problem is a fear of rejection, so these individuals adapt their behaviour to fit in perfectly.

The most obvious problem with defining abnormal using social norms is that there are cultural differences, and there is no universal agreement over what is normal and abnormal. Henlin (1964) compared the example of suicide in Scandinavia and the reasons for it. In Sweden, the suicide rate was high because of self-hatred at failing to attain ambiguous goals, while in Norway, the rate is low because suicide is associated with the loss of a loved one only.

Different societies have different beliefs about the origins of illness and thus of normal behaviour. The Dobu (New Guinea) see illness as due to the loss of soul – that is, the soul has become separated from the body leading to wasting diseases. The Yoruba (Nigeria) believe in a disease called 'maagua', which afflicts men who have affairs with other men's wives. Finally, the Azande (North Africa) talk of 'mangu'. This is a substance found inside the bodies of certain people, and is the cause of pain and distress in

Cannibalism

There are two distinct types of cannibalism associated either with 'mortuary rites' or 'warfare'.

- The former type is the eating of the flesh of the dead kin or group members in order to 'incorporate' the dead person. This is known as 'endocannibalism'.
- The latter type is known is 'exocannibalism'. It is used as the sign of ultimate victory – that is, to eat the flesh of the dead enemy.

The best reported historical case of these practices is from the Kuru (New Guinea).

C Seymour-Smith, *Macmillan Dictionary of Anthropology*, 1986, Palgrave, Reproduced with permission of Palgrave.

'Liget'

Rosaldo (1984) has studied the Ilongot (New Guinea) who believe that anger can be 'forgotten' if it is 'paid for'. The Ilongot call this 'liget', and it is a distinct possession of men.

'A young Ilongot possessed by liget might weep or sing or sulk. He might stop eating certain foods, slash baskets, yell, spill water or demonstrate imitation and distraction. And, when liget has reached its peak, he will be moved to slice the head from a neighbouring tribesman' (Gergen, 1991).

After this event the 'liget' is gone, the former sufferer is full of energy and a deepened self-knowledge, and the community may celebrate this event. The Ilongot are head-hunters and head-slicing is a common behaviour.

Wetherell and Maybin, 1996.

Figure 1.4: Cannibalism and 'liget'

others when activated by the evil thoughts of the bearer. In all these cases, the normal means of help is from a spiritual advisor – for example, a shamen (Hurd *et al*, 1986). There are other examples of such behaviour (see Figure 1.4).

Definitions of abnormality also change over time, and vary between sub-cultures. A well-known example of changing definitions of mental illness is with homosexuality. In DSM II (1968) (the American classification system of mental illness) homosexuality was classified in the category of sexual deviations. This was replaced in DSM III (1980) by the concept of ego-dystonic homosexuality (EDH) – that is, someone who is homosexually aroused, but finds it anxiety-producing, and wants to be heterosexual. DSM IV (1994) has now removed that category, and has included it in the category 'sexual disorders not otherwise specified'.

This American view contrasts with part of Melanesia (Pacific Islands) where adolescents are encouraged by their fathers to have relationships with older men (Humphreys, 1997).

In Victorian times, women wore between six to

eight undergarments to make sure that every part of their bodies – except their faces – were covered. In particular, the female leg was seen as highly arousing for men, such that even table legs were covered, and the word 'limb' was used instead of 'leg' in polite company (Kirkpatrick, 1975).

Statistical norms

Because of the subjective nature of social norms, it is felt that more objective criteria are needed. This approach takes the statistical majority of a particular behaviour to be the norm (see Figure 1.5). This can manifest itself as more frequent cases of the behaviour than the statistical mean, or the level of intensity of the behaviour. In the first case, most people may feel occasionally like another personality, but it is the frequent feelings of this that would be diagnosed as 'multiple personalities'.

Concerning the level of intensity, a majority of people experience feeling low from time to time, but it is an intense unhappiness that would be diagnosed as depression.

By far the most common statistical technique is the normal distribution. This is a statistical concept that is able to establish the scores of a majority of people on a particular test. It is most often used for intelligence. Any IQ test will have a mean score (usually standardized to 100), and a standard deviation (which shows how the scores cluster around the mean).

It has been statistically established that certain percentages of the population can be found at certain scores (standard deviations). Statistically 95% of the population will score between –2 and +2 standard deviations of the mean (see Figure 1.6). This is classed as the normal range. Using an IQ test with a standard deviation of 15, this would make the normal range vary from 70 (–2 standard deviations) to 130 (+2). Therefore, anyone with an IQ outside that

1% of Americans did not believe in God in 1989 (10% in Britain in 1998)

50% of Americans do not read books

59% of Americans are classed as overweight

94% of male Americans would change their looks if they could

58% of British households participated in the National Lottery in 1998–9

8% of men and 10% of women aged 35–44 years in Britain had no sexual partners in 1998

'Social Trends 2000', National Statistics,
© Crown Copyright 2000.

Figure 1.5: Statistical normality

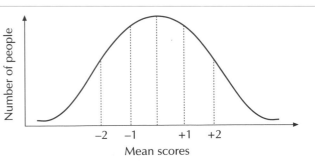

Figure 1.6: Normal distribution curve

range is classed as abnormal. In fact, on this basis the Mental Health Act of 1984 in Britain established an IQ of below 70 as 'intellectually retarded'. This appears to be much more objective than the social norm criteria.

However, this is not the case. First, IQ tests vary on their standard deviations. For example, the Stanford-Binet test has a standard deviation of 16, while for the Wechsler Adult Intelligence Scale (WAIS), it is 15. Another test may have a standard deviation of 10. In each case, there will be a different range that is classed as the normal range (see Table 1.3, below).

Second, the decision to establish the normal range as –2 to +2 standard deviations is a subjective one. It could quite easily be –1 to +1 standard deviations (which covers approximately 68% of the population), or –3 to +3 standard deviations (98% of population approximately).

Commentary

The concept of a normal distribution for intelligence was popularized by Francis Galton in the nineteenth century. He was the President of the British Eugenics Society, and was looking for scientific justification for eugenics policy, the belief that by selective breeding the population of society can be improved. The policy would involve the sterilization of women classed as 'feeble-minded' with an IQ below –2 standard deviations. This sort of idea was popular in USA in the early twentieth century and was taken to the extreme by the Nazis in Germany.

Criticisms of statistical norms

The concept of a statistical norm has been criticized generally for a number of reasons, as outlined below.

Test	A	B	C
Mean	100	100	100
Standard deviation	20	15	10
–2 to +2 range	60–140	70–130	80–120

Table 1.3: Different ranges of different IQ tests

- Behaviour at the two extremes of the normal distribution are both classed as abnormal, but are entirely different. An individual with an IQ over 130 may be a creative genius, which is usually seen as desirable. Other statistically abnormal behaviour is also desirable, like the selfless work of Mother Theresa and her mission to the poor in India. In fact, many top sports people would be classed as statistically abnormal because of their specific abilities in one particular area.

- Conversely, some behaviours may be statistically normal, but not desirable. For example, a majority of people will suffer from some form of depression at some stage in their lives. It is usually felt that depression is not a desirable or normal state of affairs. Controversially, Hassett and White (1989) suggest that more than half of the USA population have experienced abuse of some kind as a child. Again this may be statistically normal, but not desirable.

- Behaviours like intelligence are traditionally measurable by IQ tests, and the application of statistical scores and the normal distribution is possible. But other behaviours may not be so easily measurable nor conform to the normal distribution – for example, neurotic behaviour or psychoses. Often it is a combination of different behaviours together that create the problem. Many people diet regularly and are aware of the calorific value of the food they eat. But this is not the same as anorexia, which includes other behaviours such as an obsession with food.

- In some situations, like sub-cultures, deviant behaviour may in fact be the statistical norm. In a survey of 1445 London schoolboys, Belson (1975) found that the majority admitted to minor prosecutable offences (like shoplifting).

- Finally, as with social norms, there are no universal statistical norms, and there will be cultural differences in what behaviour the majority perform. Lee (1961) studied 616 Zulu (South African) women who had no evidence of mental problems. But, in response to unhappy events in their lives, around 50% admitted to going out by themselves to an isolated place and screaming continuously for hours, days or even weeks. Around 30% of the women also reported seeing 'angels'. However, for many societies, such as the Hopi Indians, hallucinations are seen as a normal part of grief.

Specific measures

This group of definitions for normality and abnormality moves away from the concept of norms and introduces specific measures. In the text that follows, four examples will be outlined:

- Maladaptive/unexpected behaviour
- Highly consistent/inconsistent
- Exposure to psychiatric treatment
- Functional/dysfunctional behaviour.

Maladaptive/unexpected behaviour

This measure is concerned with behaviour of individuals in relation to their own well-being or that of their social group – for example, individuals who consume large amounts of alcohol, such that they become addicted and cannot function properly in their jobs. However, it could be argued that alcoholism is a means of coping with unpleasant circumstances. Alexander (1990) argues that drug addiction is a rational coping mechanism for individuals unemployed and living in poverty. The reason behind the behaviour is seen as 'integration failure'. Some individuals are not able to integrate (to fit in) to society for whatever reason, and thus become isolated. Alexander believes that in this case 'the banal, mind-numbing addict culture is more bearable than isolation' (quoted in Toates, 1996, p. 39).

Unfortunately, this approach is a version of the norms mentioned earlier. It assumes that certain behaviour is expected or adaptive in a particular situation.

Commentary

RD Laing argued that the behaviour of schizophrenics was adaptive from their point of view. It is a journey of self-discovery that individuals should be allowed to undertake, regardless of what other people say. In some situations, particularly when society is unjust, maladaptive behaviour is a good thing. In nineteenth-century America, slaves who ran away from their masters were showing maladaptive behaviour as far as the slave masters viewed it. But it seems like a normal desire to be free.

There are also the problems associated with norms, including cultural differences.

Highly consistent/inconsistent

This is a very similar attempt to find specific measures. So individuals who show consistent behaviour where flexibility is required, or who are inconsistent when stability is required, would be defined as abnormal. The first case can be seen in autism. Here the same rigid repetitive behaviour is shown in all situations, and the child becomes distressed if the ritual is varied. Meanwhile, the second case could be seen in manic depressives. Sufferers alternate in a relatively short time between mania and depression. This definition is very difficult to actually measure in practice.

Exposure to psychiatric treatment

This measure can be seen as fairly accurate. Anybody who seeks psychiatric help, in whatever form (for example, from a psychiatrist, a therapist or through counselling) is classed as abnormal. The figures can quite easily be collected from records of psychiatrists and so on.

However, the most striking problem with this approach is that some people who have psychological problems never seek treatment, and some individuals will seek help even if there is no real problem. For example, among certain social groups in New York it is fashionable to have psychoanalysis. Thus people may be visiting an analyst because of the social pressure to do so. With this definition of normality, there is also the problem that diagnosis of psychological problems and referral for psychiatric help is not an exact science. It may involve mistakes or even bias.

Commentary

Pilgrim and Rogers (1993) argue that the process of diagnosing mental illness is biased against women. In England in 1986, 29% more women than men were diagnosed as being mentally ill. This is not because more women are mentally ill, but that the diagnosis system is biased (see Key Study 2).

KEY STUDY 2

Researchers: Broverman *et al* (1970)

Aim: To discover what is viewed as normal or abnormal behaviour.

Method: The researchers asked 79 mental health professionals to describe either a normal adult male, a normal adult female or a normal adult using a list of characteristics supplied by the experimenter.

Results: Most of the responses described the normal male and the normal adult in the same way. In particular, they were seen as competent, while the normal adult female was seen as submissive and concerned about her appearance.

Conclusions: Many stereotypes of normal behaviour are assumed to be male, and those of abnormal to be female.

Functional/dysfunctional behaviour

This definition is very similar to the idea of consistent and inconsistent behaviour. In trying to define what is functional or dysfunctional behaviour, it becomes a subjective exercise. However, there are some claims that objective measures are possible. Padesky (1990) quotes work by Strickland comparing depressed and non-depressed individuals under stress. The depressed individuals showed an exaggerated physiological reaction to the stress.

Whether a behaviour is functional or dysfunctional depends on the viewpoint of the observer or the actor of the behaviour. Rosenhan and Seligman (1995) point out that there will be differences in the information about the behaviour, knowledge of its frequency and the standards imposed about the behaviour. For example, the actors know why they do the behaviour, how often it occurs, and how their own standards account for the behaviour. So to them there is nothing wrong. But observers do not know why the behaviour occurs, nor how often, and it may conflict with their own standards. Therefore, for them, the behaviour is dysfunctional.

None of these specific measures is adequate to help us define normality and abnormality, and who needs help.

Subjective assessment

This group of approaches to defining what is normal and abnormal concentrates on the feelings of the individuals themselves or those around them – for example:

- personal distress
- others' distress
- understanding in relation to the self.

Personal distress

This definition can be summarized as either that individuals feel there is something wrong (distressing) about their own behaviour or that they fail to live up to their own standards (Shoben, 1957).

Warr and Payne (1982) asked a sample of British people: 'did you experience unpleasant emotional strain yesterday?' Some 65% replied 'Not at all', while 4% said 'All of the time' and 5% 'Most of the time'; the rest were 'Little or some of the time'. So, by the personal distress definition, the 9% who said 'all or most of the time' would be classed as having problems. But how do we know if people are being honest in their replies? They may have directly lied or not remembered accurately how they had felt.

The other problems with this definition include the fact that two people may react differently. At the first sign of unhappiness, some people will feel uneasy, while others may live their lives unhappy and feel nothing is wrong.

However, for some people, they may be happy but their behaviour is disturbing to others. One of the criteria for assessing psychosis is that the individual does not believe there is a problem, as well as outright denial of the problem. One of the first steps in treatment of alcoholism is the admittance of an alcohol problem.

Commentary

Because we live in a society with expectations and norms, people may become distressed that they do not live up to what is expected, without there really being a problem. For example, in Western society, great emphasis is placed on physical appearance, particularly for women. Many women are unhappy with their appearance and seek cosmetic surgery when there is not really a problem.

Others' distress

Alternatively, we could try to measure abnormal behaviour by the distress it causes other people. However, two people can vary very much in what they find distressing, and this definition is no better than that of social norms.

Understanding in relation to the self

One criterion may be the level of understanding that an individual has about him or herself. Those with low self-awareness – particularly of distressing behaviour – are seen as having problems. But as mentioned earlier, the denial of there being a problem is a symptom of some illnesses.

Furthermore, individual levels of self-awareness vary. One person may, for example, be unaware that he (or she) is tactless and says the wrong thing in social situations. This may be distressing, but not necessarily a sign of mental problems. You may say that social skills should be appropriate to the situation, but that becomes a subjective decision.

Mental health criterion

This approach to defining what is normal and abnormal concentrates on the ideal – that is, what is necessary to be mentally healthy. It is used in the same way as we talk about physical health. Thus anybody who does not fit the characteristics of being mentally healthy is classed as having problems.

The issue, then, is how to define what is mentally healthy. A number of researchers have tried to

Characteristic	Jahoda (1958)	Wright *et al* (1978)	Rosenhan and Seligman (1995)	Atkinson *et al* (1990)
Number of behaviours	8	7	7*	5
1 Absence of mental illness; not suffering or showing discomfort	Y		YY	
2 Ability to introspect; show self-knowledge and rational behaviour	Y		Y	Y
3 Personal growth; self-actualization; happiness	Y	Y		
4 Integration, balance and equilibrium; self-esteem; lack of guilt; conventional	Y	Y	Y	Y
5 Ability to cope with stress; lack of anxiety	Y	Y		
6 Autonomy (independent and able to control own behaviour); maturity; not violating own standards	Y	Y	YY	Y
7 Realistic view of world; adjusted; adaptive to life	Y	Y	Y	Y
8 Abilities to work, love and play; 'efficient'	Y	YY		Y

* Rosenhan and Seligman's criteria are for abnormality that has been turned around; YY = characteristics appearing as two criteria in that definition of mental health

Table 1.4: Different definitions of mental health

establish the criteria. Table 1.4, on the previous page, outlines the four main definitions used.

Generally the definitions can be integrated to give an overview of what are seen as the characteristics of mental health.

1 The individual is not suffering from mental illness or discomfort.
2 The individual is able to reflect on his (or her) behaviour, and to be rational about what he/she does or who he/she is.
3 The individual has personal growth, and/or happiness, which is shown by self-actualization. Self-actualization is 'becoming everything that one is capable of becoming' (Maslow, 1970).
4 The individual is integrated, balanced and in equilibrium. All these terms are used to mean he or she has a sound self-esteem, a lack of guilt, and is probably conventional. There are no obvious signs of the individual's personality fragmenting.
5 This is the ability to cope with stress and to show a lack of anxiety.
6 Autonomy refers to the individual being independent of others and able to control his (or her) own behaviour. This shows itself in maturity, and not violating his own moral standards.
7 The individual has a realistic view of the world, to which he/she is adjusted or adapted.
8 Finally, this is the ability to work, love (that is, have intimate relationships), and play (that is, enjoy non-work activities). This is called 'efficiency' by some.

This approach concentrates on the definition of what is mentally healthy as these criteria show. But in practice, the criteria are far too idealistic and hardly anyone would be mentally healthy. For example, 'the ability to cope with stress' does not say how the person copes, nor does it give the level of stress. Some people cope by denying the stress and some stress levels are so high that coping is not possible. Furthermore, Scott (1958) points out that any criteria 'based on adjustment clearly implies that conformity to the social situation in which the individual is permanently embedded is a healthy response'. So, in fact, conformity is being seen as normal and healthy, but it may be non-conformists who can challenge society and are achieving self-actualization.

Though the mental health criterion appears objective, it is quite subjective in what it does and does not include. For example, the concepts of per-

sonal growth and self-actualization are difficult to pin down. Simply, they suggest that the individual is fulfilling his or her potential a large amount of the time, or moving towards that potential. Everyday life can be very mundane and people are nowhere near such grand ideas. It puts great pressure on people to be achieving so much most of the time.

As with most definitions, there will be cultural differences in what is classed as healthy or not (see RLA 4). Manifestations of problems vary between cultures – for example, catatonic stupor is rare in the West, but common in Asia. One reason could be that Eastern religions advocate withdrawal as a response to difficulties and that is seen as mentally healthy there.

Another example can be seen in the traditional Japanese attitudes towards suicide. Ritual suicide is seen as an honourable response when the individual has failed completely in his or her duties and obligations. An Innuit mother, on the other hand, accepts her son's killer as a replacement for the dead child rather than try to punish the murderer.

Commentary

Some problems are found in some cultures only. For example, 'latah' found in Malaysia, is triggered by fright usually among low status individuals. They start to mimic others of higher status, mumble indistinctly, and use curses and obscenities a lot.

Real Life Application 4:

Worldwide definition of mentally healthy

Dr. Sartorius of the World Health Organization makes the following points about attempting to establish worldwide criteria for measuring mental health.

- Mental health is not just the absence of illness. Individuals may not be mentally ill, yet not necessarily mentally healthy at the same time.
- One way of assessing mental health is as a state of balance between the individual and the environment. This is often used as a model for stress. The individual has certain resources to deal with stress, and until stress reaches beyond a certain level, there is no problem.
- Traditional indicators, like suicide rate, are limited in the accuracy they provide of a society's mental health.
- An individual's mental health is also influenced by the society as a whole. The factors involved include the economic prosperity of the society

and the general 'quality of life'. That does not mean that wealth equals mental health. In the 1980s, the Venezuelan government decided to increase the level of education of the general population by specific programmes under the Ministry of Intelligence, so that the citizens could benefit from the country's democracy.

Adapted from 'What is mental health?', *All in the Mind*, BBC Radio 4, 1991.

Summary

- An individual's mental health is not only the absence of mental illness. It is also the state of balance between the individual and the environment, and the society in which he/she lives.

Questions

1 Other than those mentioned in RLA 4, what traditional indicators of a society's mental health are used?

2 Why is the society we live in important for our mental health?

3 What mental health benefits would a more educated Venezuelan society gain?

Mental illness

This is the current definition used in Western psychiatry today. The full details of this view, sometimes known as the medical or biomedical model, will be discussed in Chapter 2 (see pages 15–26).

The main point of this definition is that the individual who is abnormal has an illness – that is, something physically wrong. There is a parallel with physical illness. Historically many physical explanations have been sought (see RLA 5).

Real Life Application 5:

What is madness?

'Throughout history, people's understanding of madness and sanity has constantly shifted. Different cultures have perceived as mad those whom others might call sane. The treatments received by the mad have been determined by whatever theory of madness has at that time been dominant.'

Historically, there have been attempts to locate a definite cause for abnormal behaviour. Initially, the concept of possession was used, and is still used in some cultures today. It is based on the assumption that everything or everyone has a soul which could be possessed by evil spirits. This was particularly seen in the Middle Ages in witch trials. Deutsch (1949) estimates 100 000 people (mainly women) died at witch trials in Europe and the American colonies between the mid 15th and 17th centuries.

One response to possession was to drill a small hole in the skull of the victim to allow the evil spirit to escape. This is known as trepanning, and is still used today in some cultures, but very rarely.

Other physical causes include a roaming uterus (Ancient Greece) or the disturbance of the four humours in the body: black bile, yellow bile, blood and phlegm (Hippocrates). For the Victorians, madness was primarily a female experience linked to childbirth or 'lactational insanity' (poor mothers who breast-fed for long periods to save money and prevent conception). It was not until World War I that it was realized that men could experience hysteria based on what happened in the trenches.

Herman and Green, 1991.

Summary

- Throughout history different explanations have been used for madness and unusual behaviour. The traditional explanations have included possession by evil spirits.

Questions

1 Is trepanning a physical treatment or a therapy?

2 Why did the attitude towards hysteria change after the First World War?

3 What does the idea of the 'roaming uterus' suggest about madness?

Legal implications

The use of mental illness as the modern means of defining abnormality has a very important consequence – legal backing. In England and Wales, Mental Health Acts have been passed that influence the powers given to psychiatrists – in particular, the Mental Health Act of 1983 as it stands at the moment.

Part 1 of this Act laid out a legal definition of mental disorder: 'Mental illness, arrested or incomplete development of the mind, psychopathic disorder and any other disorder or disability of the mind'.

Under part 2 of the Act, compulsory admission was introduced. This allows the detention for 72 hours for emergency treatment or up to 28 days for assessment of the individual. This can be without the consent of the individual, and based upon the decision of one or two doctors or psychiatrists. The police can also be involved in the 'removal to a place of safety from a public place' – that is, to arrest individuals who appear mentally ill (see RLA 6). Table 1.5 summarizes the compulsory admissions procedure.

Real Life Application 6:

Whose mind is it anyway?

Ghanian-born Phillip Addo is an Afro-Caribbean man living in Battersea, south London. He has changed his name to 'John Baptist' and believes that he was born with white skin. He also believes that he is heir to the Russian throne, and denies being mentally ill.

'John's' battle with the mental health system is followed in the BBC documentary *Minders*.

- 3 August 1994: police arrive at 'John's' flat for a section 2 of the Mental Health Act 1983 – that is, to compulsory detain him because he fails to care for himself but is not dangerous. 'John' feels that the drugs he is forced to take are harmful. He has delusions, but no hallucinations or other thought disorders typical of schizophrenia.
- 8 August: in hospital refusing medication and food, 'John' is given a forced injection of an anti-psychotic drug.
- 11 August: the Mental Health Review Tribunal rule that 'John' must remain in hospital, but he runs away.
- 22 August: the police find him at his flat, and he agrees to return to hospital as an 'informal patient'.
- 17 October: 'John' is allowed to leave hospital if he continues with his medication. But he wants to stop it as soon as possible because of the unpleasant side effects.

This brief extract is an example of the cycle of taking drugs and getting better, or refusing them and having problems, that occurs in 'John's' life.

Adapted from 'Whose mind is it anyway?', *Minders*, BBC, 1995.

Summary

- Phillip Addo shows many symptoms of mental illness, such as delusions, but he is not dangerous to himself or others. There is an ethical issue of whether he should be forced to take drugs, of which he does not like the side effects.

Questions

1 Give an example of a delusion by 'John'.

2 What is the everyday term for being detained under section 2 of the Mental Health Act 1983?

3 Under what part of the Mental Health Act can the police arrest 'John'?

Distinctions in the Mental Health Act

While in hospital, the Mental Health Act distinguishes between informal and formal patients, and their rights to refuse treatment. Informal patients – that is, those who voluntarily admit themselves to a psychiatric hospital – have the right to refuse treatment (except in an emergency). Formal patients – that is, those who are admitted without consent,

Purpose	Who	Applicant	Duration
Assessment	2 doctors	ASW/NR	28 days
Treatment	2 doctors	ASW/NR	6 months
Urgent assessment from community	1 doctor	ASW/NR	72 hours
Urgent detention of in-patient	1 doctor	–	72 hours
Removal to place of safety from public place	police	–	72 hours

ASW = 'approved' social worker under Mental Health Act
NR = nearest relative

Table 1.5: Compulsory admissions procedure under Mental Health Act 1983

known as 'sectioned' – in theory have the same rights, but this consent can be circumvented by two doctors. Under section 62 of the Act, doctors can take action without consent to save the patient's life, to stop his (or her) condition deteriorating seriously, to reduce serious suffering, to prevent the patient from behaving violently or from being a danger to himself/others. The main method used here would be the administering of drugs without consent, though electro-convulsive therapy (ECT) can also be used.

The mental health users' movement is not, surprisingly, critical of these powers. This movement is made up of individuals who have been through the psychiatric system, and many feel the powers are misused. Peter Campbell, who sees himself as a 'survivor' of the mental health system, has reservations about 'deterioration in health' as a criteria for forced treatment. He gives the example of an individual who ignores advice after a heart attack. Applying the criteria of the Mental Health Act to this situation, doctors would stop such a person from smoking, eating unhealthy food and so on – in other words, take away their 'free will' (Peter Campbell speaking on *All in the Mind*, 1995).

Attitudes towards mental illness

The diagnosis of a person as mentally ill also has social implications. In the main, the image portrayed by the media of mental illness is very negative and it leads to the stigmatization of sufferers.

Vousden (1989) points out that the tabloid newspapers enrich their headlines with adjectives associated with mental health problems, like 'loony left'. Terms like 'paranoid schizophrenia' are used inaccurately and to cover any sufferer of mental illness who is different.

There is an overemphasis on violence, and stories about the special psychiatric hospitals, like Broadmoor, which are for offenders. The Glasgow University Media Group (1993) analysed the representations of mental illness on television, and in newspapers and magazines during one month in 1993. Of approximately 500 fictional representations of mental illness, over 300 referred to harm to others by the sufferer, and of the 70 factual representations, 50 were the same. Thus the message is that mental illness sufferers will harm others. But, in reality, this is rare. The greatest risk is that sufferers will harm themselves.

In a MORI survey in 1996, as part of the BBC season entitled 'States of mind', a quarter of respondents said they would rather admit to having a life-threatening disease than to be suffering from mental illness.

Yarney (1999) surveyed 1737 people in the UK about their attitudes to the different types of mental illness. The vast majority saw sufferers of schizophrenia and drug addiction as dangerous, but not eating disorder sufferers.

Conclusions

Smith *et al* (1986) emphasize that no one definition is sufficient by itself to define normality and abnormality because the behaviour of individuals with behaviour disorders 'is maladaptive because it is inflexible and unrealistic. It is also likely to be statistically uncommon and socially deviant, although neither of these characteristics is always present. People whose behaviour is abnormal may or may not seem unhappy about their failure to adapt.'

Essay questions

1 Discuss, with reference to the implications, the different definitions of normality and abnormality.

2 'There is no universal definition of normality.' Discuss.

3 Discuss the different definitions of normality and abnormality, with particular reference to cultural differences.

2 Approaches to abnormal behaviour

This chapter looks at the five most important models of mental disorders – the medical model, the behavioural model, the psychodynamic model, the cognitive model and the humanistic model.

Real Life Applications that are considered are:

- RLA 7: Diagnosing mental illness
- RLA 8: Labelling and stigma
- RLA 9: Culture bound syndromes
- RLA 10: Koro
- RLA 11: Non-Western approaches to abnormal behaviour

As with the definitions of normality and abnormality (discussed in Chapter 1), there are many approaches to mental disorders. Each approach, or model, sees the cause of the mental disorders as being different and also how that model would treat it.

Medical model

This model is by far the most important approach to abnormality because it is the one that dominates Western psychiatry today. It is also known as the biomedical model and somatic, or physical, approach. The basis of this model is that the cause of the mental disorder or problem is an illness – that is, mental illness. There are three main assumptions, which will be outlined first then explored in detail.

- Assumption 1: abnormal behaviour can be classified into syndromes or groups of behaviours occurring together.
- Assumption 2: all symptoms reflect an underlying physiological disease.
- Assumption 3: treatment is by physical means only.

Assumption 1

The assumption that abnormal behaviour can be classified into syndromes or groups of behaviours occurring together has led to the classification systems, which are the basis of modern diagnosis. At the beginning of the twentieth century, Emil Kraeplin noted the frequency with which certain signs and symptoms occurred together. This suggested to him that the symptoms could be classed as 'diseases' or 'syndromes' (sets of symptoms) (see Figure 2.1).

This basic observation was developed into the classification system, where diagnosis is based on signs and symptoms of the illness. This gives a prognosis (that is, a forecast or prediction) that follows from the diagnosis and may be based on experience from a large number of similar cases.

All the modern classification systems stem from

The word 'psychiatry' appeared in the English language in 1846; 'psychosis' appeared in 1847 and 'paranoia' in 1857.

From 1900 the psychiatric landscape underwent an 'almost volcanic geological upheaval'. The many different types of mental disorder were grouped into two 'snowcapped peaks' – manic depression, and schizophrenia (as it became called by Eugen Bleuler in 1911) became the 'psychiatry Everest'.

David Hill, who is critical of the medical model, argues that in the late nineteenth century psychiatry was struggling to justify itself compared to progress being made in other sciences. New terms like 'dementia praecox' gave psychiatry a new language, which helped it gain control over the understanding and treatment of madness.

But in the original list of symptoms of schizophrenia, Kraeplin included some very Victorian concerns – for example, 'rude to their superiors', 'smokes a cigar in church', 'wears a hat in church' and 'wears unwashed and dirty clothes'.

Jonathan Miller, *Madness*, 'In two minds', 1991.

Figure 2.1: Kraeplin's categories

Emil Kraeplin

the work of Emil Kraeplin. In the USA, psychiatrists use the *American Psychiatric Association's Diagnostic and Statistical Manual of Mental Disorders* (DSM). This was first formulated in 1952. Since then it has been revised in 1968, 1980, 1987 and lastly in 1994 as DSM IV. In the UK, psychiatrists use a similar system called ICD 10 (1987). This is the *Mental Disorders Section of the 10th Revision of the International Classification of Disease by the World Health Organization* (see RLA 7). Tables 2.1 and 2.2 give more details of DSM IV and ICD 10.

Real Life Application 7:
Diagnosing mental illness

Case 1

John has brief periods of happiness, but most of the time he is afraid of the voice that keeps saying 'useless'. He is concerned about an organ, close to the heart, which had been implanted secretly in his body. It transmitted all his thoughts back to the central headquarters. He believed that his thoughts could affect the future of the world.

Case 2

Jane is often overcome by a fear of not being clean and that her dirtiness would infect other people. This lead to an excessive washing of her hands in a particular way. Then she was troubled by thoughts that she had not turned the taps off properly. Consequently she would spend many hours in the bathroom checking, even though she could see no water coming out of the taps.

Case 3

Mary is generally doing well at university, both in terms of her work and her relationships. But she is anxious about what to do after she finishes her course. She seeks advice from careers officers and her friends. Most of her friends have similar concerns.

Questions

1 Look at the symptoms described for each individual and, based on the DSM IV criteria, decide what mental illness would be diagnosed.

Diagnosis with DSM IV is based on five axes, as outlined below.

Axis I: clinical disorders – all recognized clinical syndromes except personality disorders and mental retardation.

1 Disorders usually first diagnosed in infancy, childhood or adolescence – e.g. Attention Deficit Hyperactivity Disorder (ADHD), Conduct Disorders (CD).

2 Organic mental disorders – e.g. senile dementia, Alzheimer's disease.

3 Substance-related disorders – e.g. alcoholism; drug addiction.

4 Schizophrenia and other psychotic disorders.

5 Mood disorders – e.g. depression, mania.

6 Anxiety disorders – e.g. phobias, Panic Disorder.

7 Somatoform disorders – e.g. Body Dysmorphic Disorder.

8 Dissociative disorder – e.g. Dissociative Identity Disorder.

9 Sexual and gender-identity disorders.

Axis II: personality disorders and adult mental retardation

Axis III: general medical condition – i.e., non-mental medical disorders that are potentially relevant (e.g. heart attack; diabetes in children with enuresis).

Axis IV: psychosocial and environmental problems – severity of psychosocial stressors in last year on scale 1 (none) to 6 (catastrophe – e.g. multiple family deaths).

Axis V: global assessment of functioning.

Level of functioning and symptoms on scale of 1 to100

100 = superior functioning in range of activities

 90 = absent or minimal symptoms

 80 = symptoms transient and reaction to stress

 70 = some mild symptoms and functioning problems

60 = moderate symptoms

50 = serious symptoms and impairment of functioning

40 = some impairment in reality testing

30 = behaviour influenced by hallucinations and so on

20 = some danger of hurting self or others

10 = persistent danger of hurting self or others

1 = extreme danger of hurting self or others

Table 2.1: DSM IV

F00–09: Organic mental disorders

e.g. dementia with Alzheimer late onset

e.g. delirium

F10–19: Mental and behavioural disorders due to psychoactive substance use

e.g. alcohol

F20–29: Schizophrenia, schizotypal and delusional disorders

e.g. paranoid schizophrenia

F30–39: Affective (mood) disorders

e.g. Recurrent Depressive Disorder

F40–48: Neurotic, stress-related and somatoform disorders

e.g. Post-Traumatic Stress Disorder

e.g. Conversion Disorder

e.g. Multiple Personality Disorder

F50–59: Behavioural syndromes association with physiological disturbance and physical factors

e.g. anxiety

e.g. sexual dysfunction

F60–69: Disorders of adult personality and behaviour

F70–79: Mental retardation

F80–89: Disorders of psychological development

e.g. childhood autism

F90–98: Behavioural and emotional disorders with onset usually occurring in childhood or adolescence

e.g. Hyperkinetic Disorder

e.g. Separation Anxiety Disorder

e.g. pica

F99 Unspecified mental disorder

Table 2.2: ICD-10 categories

Commentary

Phillip Zimbardo (1987) gives four reasons why it is necessary to classify and diagnose mental illness:

1 To plan appropriate treatment.

2 For the legal aspect of competency to stand trial.

3 For research and evaluation purposes.

4 For economic reasons – that is, payment for those unable to work.

Assumption 2

The assumption that all symptoms reflect an underlying physiological disease sees all mental illness as having a physical cause. Baron (1985) calls it an 'anatomicopathologic fact' – in other words, mental illness is an 'objective entity' located somewhere in the body. Thus it excludes the social and psychological dimensions of the illness, and ignores the meaning of the disease to the individual. For the psychiatrist, diagnosis is a factual account.

Commentary

Why do psychiatrists ignore the personal experience of the patients in diagnosis? According to Donnelly (1988), the reasons are as follows.

- It is not part of the medical tradition to ask about patients' feelings.
- Modern technology in diagnosis has removed the need to use patients' views.
- Asking patients' feelings seems too subjective.

The main causes of mental illness are seen to be germs, genes, neurochemistry (chemistry of the brain) or neuroanatomy (the structure of the brain – for example, minor brain damage). Details of these causes as applied to specific mental illnesses are studied further in Chapter 3.

Assumption 3

If the cause of the mental illness is physical, then the treatment must also be physical. The medical model focuses on the use of psychotrophic drugs, electroconvulsive therapy (ECT) and psychosurgery. Each of these techniques causes a physical intervention in the body. Details of these methods are found in Chapter 4 (see pages 64–9).

Strengths of the medical model

The medical model dominates psychiatry today. Compared to other models, it has both strengths and weaknesses. Its main strength is that it concentrates on diagnosis in order to help find the appropriate treatment. By assuming that patients, though relatively unique, are similar in their symptoms, past experience can help in the treatment of current problems. For example, what has worked for schizophrenia in the past may also help today.

To view the problem as mental illness is more humane than to see the person as morally defective or guilty, which was the view taken before the twentieth century. Thus there is a concept of 'no blame', just the aim to cure. It is not the person's fault if he or she suffers from, say, schizophrenia.

The diagnosis system itself uses jargon terms, but it is possible for all to see how the diagnosis was arrived at. Each illness will have 'essential features' – in other words, symptoms that are the basis of the defining of the illness. Then there will be 'associated features' – that is, symptoms that are usually present with a particular mental illness. The 'diagnostic criteria' are the symptoms that are used to diagnose the mental illness. Finally, 'differential diagnosis' helps distinguish one mental illness from another that has similar symptoms.

Problems with the medical model

The medical model and psychiatry is not without its critics and problems. The main area of issue is the classification systems, but also the causes of the mental illnesses.

Reliability

For the classification systems to be trusted, they must show reliability. This takes two forms:

- inter-judge reliability
- test-retest reliability.

With inter-judge reliability, two different psychiatrists must independently give the same diagnosis, based on the same symptoms. Most of the research to test this type of reliability uses mock case studies for psychiatrists to diagnose (that is, they do not actually meet a patient).

Earlier research, using less specific categories of mental illness before DSM III (1980), found little reliability. Schmidt and Fonda (1956) asked two psychiatrists to diagnose independently 426 patients. There was great variety in the diagnoses between the psychiatrists, especially for patients with schizophrenia. However, Beck et al (1962) found between 50%–80% agreement on diagnoses by four psychiatrists with 153 patients. However, where the studies have used real patients, it has been found that different interviewers extracted different answers from the same patients, and this accounted for some of the differences in diagnosis (Word et al, 1952).

More recently, in a large-scale study of psychiatrists in nine countries on the diagnosis of schizophrenia, the World Health Organization (1973) found substantial agreement between psychiatrists in Columbia, Czechoslovakia, Denmark, England, India, Nigeria and Taiwan, but not with the USA or USSR.

The second type of reliability is test-retest reliability, which involves the same patients being diagnosed the same at two different times by the same psychiatrist. The way to study this issue is by using real patients who have been readmitted to the same or another psychiatric hospital, and to compare the diagnosis given on both occasions.

Kendall (1974) studied 1913 patients admitted to hospital since 1964, and then readmitted after 1969. The research found that schizophrenia was more often rediagnosed as a form of depression than the other way around. There was a 70% stability in the diagnosis of depression, schizophrenia, dementia and alcoholism, but less than 50% stability in the diagnosis of anxiety states, paranoid states, mania and personality disorders. Often, paranoid states were rediagnosed as schizophrenia, confusional states as dementia and anxiety or phobia as depression.

Cooper (1967) looked at 200 patients in England and Wales who were readmitted to psychiatric hospitals on four separate occasions in the 1950s. Some 54% were given the same diagnosis on all four occasions.

Rosenhan and Seligman (1995) summarize the agreement coefficients for diagnosis of the main mental disorders. The disorders listed below received a code '1' (that is, an agreement coefficient of 0.75 or more: 75%+ agreement):

- organic disorders
- substance use
- schizophrenic disorders
- some affective disorders.

Childhood disorders and anxiety disorders received a '2' (moderate agreement of between 0.60 and 0.74), while some personality disorders received only a '3' (between 0.40 to 0.59 agreement coefficient). None of the main disorders received '4' (below 0.40).

Cooper (1983) concludes that the newest classification systems leave little room for subjective judgement, and thus the reliability of the diagnosis is high.

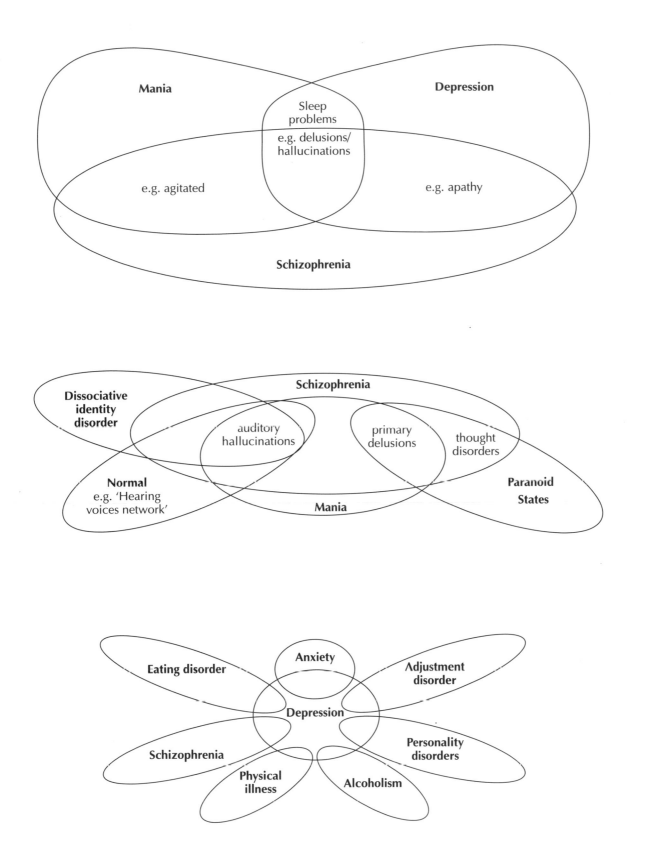

Figure 2.2: Examples of symptom overlaps

Validity

Validity is concerned with whether the classification of symptoms actually shows an underlying illness. Just because the classification systems say, for example, that thought disorders and primary delusions are the symptoms of schizophrenia, it does not mean that there is an underlying illness known as schizophrenia.

There are different types of validity, as follows.

- Aetiological validity: this type of validity looks at the historical antecedents for the disorder – that is, the cause of the disorder is the same for all sufferers.
- Concurrent validity: there are common characteristics among all sufferers of the same disorder. Schizophrenics, for example, can have very different symptoms between type I and type II schizophrenia.
- Predictive validity: it is possible to predict the future outcomes of the illness from the diagnosis.
- Descriptive validity: there will be differences in the symptoms of the patients within the different sub-categories of the same general diagnostic category.

One of the main questions studied by researchers is whether the symptoms used to diagnose a disorder actually show an underlying illness. The findings tend to support the diagnosis of the general categories of mental disorders, like depression, but not placing the patient in the appropriate sub-category of depression. This is the feeling for schizophrenia and personality disorders, in particular. Figure 2.2 (see page 19) gives examples of symptom overlaps.

Using the DSM III criteria, Tyrer *et al* (1988) studied the diagnosis of neurotic disorders (called anxiety disorders today). There is overlap in terms of symptoms between phobias, general anxiety disorders, obsessive-compulsive disorders, depression, somatoform disorders, some personality disorders and some eating disorders. Concentrating on 201 patients diagnosed with specific anxiety disorders, they found a mixture of sub-category diagnoses. The results are summarized in Table 2.3.

However, in defence of the validity of the classification systems, Clare (1980) points out that the diagnosis of physical illness is not always clear-cut and has similar problems.

Commentary

There is some concern with the validity of the classifica-

Actual diagnosis	General Anxiety Disorder	Panic Disorder
Number of patients	65	73
General Anxiety Disorder	45	25
Simple phobia	16	15
Social phobia	3	4
Panic Disorder	0	9
Simple and social phobia	1	4
Simple phobia and panic disorders	0	3
Dysthymia (depression)	0	7
Dysthymia and social phobia	0	2
Simple and social phobia and Panic Disorder and dysthymia	0	4

Tyrer, 1991.

Table 2.3: Summary of some of the findings by Tyrer *et al* (1988)

tion systems for female patients. This is particularly the case with personality disorders. Prentice (1996) points out that males are more often diagnosed as narcissistic personality and obsessive-compulsive personality, while females are more frequently diagnosed as histrionic personality and dependent personality.

General problems with diagnoses

Whatever the classification system used, there is the argument that psychiatrists cannot tell who is mentally ill and who is not. This argument is based on the work of David Rosenhan, who was a professor of psychiatry at Stanford University in the USA (see Key Study 3, page 21).

After the findings of Rosenhan (1973), the psychiatric hospitals involved were warned that in the following six months there would be other 'pseudo-patients'. In fact there were none. But of 193 patients, 41 were seen as 'fake' and turned away (Rosenhan 1975). However, Spitzer (1976) has criticized Rosenhan's work for the use of deception, and a limited number of 'pseudo-patients' from which to generalize.

One effect of classification systems and the process of diagnosis is labelling. Rosenhan and Seligman (1994) argue that 'society stigmatizes ordinary people who have sought psychiatric care, often to the disadvantage of both the individual and society'. Sayce (1999) quotes the case of Dawn Collins,

KEY STUDY 3

Researcher: Rosenhan (1973)

Aim: To get individuals who were not mentally ill admitted to psychiatric hospitals and for them to observe the behaviour of the staff towards the patients.

Method: Between 1969 and 1972, 8 'pseudo-patients' (Rosenhan and his students) approached 12 psychiatric hospitals reporting that they were hearing voices that said 'empty', 'dull' or 'thud'. Otherwise, they told the truth (except for using pseudonyms) and acted normally. All were admitted to a psychiatric hospital and 95% were diagnosed as schizophrenic. This study was a participant observation.

Results: The 'pseudo-patients' recorded the behaviour of the staff towards the patients, and found an average of 6 minutes each day of interaction between the staff and patients. Only 2% of the staff paused to chat with the patients. The patients were made powerless; they were depersonalized or dehumanized as a condition, rather than treated as a person. Rosenhan called the hospitals 'storehouses for the unwanted'. Of the 118 patients, 35 voiced suspicion that the 'pseudo-patients' were not really mentally ill, but none of the staff raised any suspicions. Eventually, the 'pseudo-patients' were released with 'schizophrenia in remission' still on their records – that is, the psychiatrists would not admit they were wrong.

Conclusions: Two main conclusions are drawn from this study: first, that the staff paid little attention to the patients and, second, the staff were not able to recognize a 'pseudo-patient' from a real patient.

who was raped in 1996. Her case was dropped because she was found to have a history of mental health problems. Thus she was seen (labelled) as an 'unreliable witness'.

The concept of mental illness removes any ambiguity and places the label of 'sick' on the patient. This can help the patient cope with his or her symptoms, but labelling can lead to a self-fulfilling prophecy – that is, if someone is told they are mad they may become mad (see RLA 8).

Real Life Application 8: Labelling and stigma

Labels are definitions, and when applied to people it identifies what they are. That is a 'what' rather than a 'who'. The label is associated with deviancy when the behaviour violates 'taken-for-granted' rules.

The most negative aspect of labelling is that of stigma. Jones et al (1984) define stigma as a 'mark' that sets the person out from others because they have undesirable characteristics. This leads to rejection. If a person is hospitalized for mental illness, they are thus labelled and stigmatized as 'dangerous, incompetent and untrustworthy'.

But Scheff (1966) argues that many supposed 'inappropriate behaviours' are quite common, but if these behaviours come from a labelled person, then it is a confirmation of that label. Many people, for example, like science fiction and will talk about the ideas as if they were real. But a mentally ill person doing the same would be confirming [his or her] delusional label.

Handbook of the Sociology of Mental Health, 1972.

Summary

• People become defined by their label, as a 'what' rather than a 'who'. Thus, for a person who is labelled 'mentally ill', all his or her behaviour is seen as confirming this label.

Questions

1 Give an example of a stigma about mental illness that is commonly reported.

2 Give an example of a behaviour that is often seen as a sign of mental illness, but many people have that behaviour.

> **3** Give an example of a current behaviour that is becoming acceptable, though it could be seen as a sign of mental illness

Support of labelling

Goffman (1961) talks about the labelling of 'insane' and the consequent socialization into madness by the family, police, psychiatrists and even the individual him or herself. Mental illness becomes their 'career'. However, there is little empirical support for labelling creating the problem. Lindsay (1982) set up an experiment with a group of psychiatrists. They were shown a short video of either a person diagnosed as schizophrenic or not. Different groups were either given no information about the diagnosis, the correct diagnosis or misleading information. Overwhelmingly, the schizophrenic video was diagnosed as abnormal, regardless of the information given.

Commentary

The consultation between the psychiatrist and the patient has expectations and roles, and thus cannot be neutral. Psychiatrists takes the 'expert role' – that is, they are in the position of power based on the diagnosis they can give and its consequent effect on the life of the patient. Just using the term 'patient' sets the individual in the 'sick role', and it emphasizes the 'demand characteristics' of the situation. What the psychiatrist says has to be accepted, and questions must be answered correctly by the patient. It has been argued that as soon as the individual walks through the psychiatrist's door, the situation changes and role expectations take over.

Parsons (1951) was the first to talk about the 'sick role' in reference to all medicine. It gives individuals rights like non-responsibility for their behaviour and obligations – for example, to obey the authority figures and agree with their diagnosis. Anybody who tries to resist the diagnosis process – that is, does not take on the 'sick role' – is seen as a 'difficult patient' and sanctions are imposed (like placement in a locked ward).

Duke and Nowicki (1986) highlight eight non-illness factors that influence the diagnosis process. These are:

1 Sex of the patient.
2 Ethnicity of the patient.
3 Socio-economic status of the patient.
4 Context.
5 Theoretical views of the psychiatrist.
6 Political and religious views of the patient.
7 Political and religious views of the psychiatrist.
8 Type of interview used.

Cultural differences

There are two problems here for the classification systems. First is the argument that psychiatrists in different countries will use the classification systems in different ways – that is, give different diagnoses for the same symptoms. Second is the point that mental illnesses included in the classification systems are not universal, and there are, what is called, 'culture bound syndromes' (CBS) (see RLAs 9, and 10, page 23).

Real Life Application 9:
Culture bound syndromes

After extensive research, McCajor Hall lists 36 'culture bound syndromes', which can be divided into six categories:

1 Local mental illnesses that do not have Western categories.
   Example: 'amok' found in Malaysia and Indonesia. It involves a period of brooding followed by violent behaviour. It occurs only in men.
2 Mental illnesses that resemble Western categories.
   Examples: 'taijin kyofusho' in Japan, and 'dhat' in India. 'Taijin kyofusho' is similar to the Western category of 'social phobia'. Sufferers have an intense fear that their bodies, body parts or functions are displeasing to others. 'Dhat' is a severe anxiety and hypochondria focused on the loss of semen, discoloration of urine, and feelings of weakness and exhaustion.
3 Mental illnesses not yet recognized in the West.
   Example: 'kuru', a progressive psychosis and dementia among cannibals in New Guinea. It may have similarities to Creuzfeldt-Jacob Disease (CJD).
4 Symptoms seen in many cultures, but only seen as mental illness in some.
   Examples: 'koro' and 'zar'. 'Koro' is a severe anxiety, and delusions, mainly among men, that their genitals are retracting, which leads to death. This is found in Malaysia and China. 'Zar' in North Africa is not necessarily seen as abnormal. It involves being possessed by a spirit, which causes the individual to laugh, shout, sing and weep, among other things.
5 Cultural interpretations of behaviour that are not acceptable in Western psychiatry.
   Example: 'evil eye' in Mediterranean and Middle East countries. This is used as an explanation for illness or misfortune.

6 Syndromes that do not exist.
Example: 'windigo', which is used to deal with outcasts among the Algonkian Indians. It is depression and anxiety followed by possession by a giant man-eating monster. This leads to killing and cannibalism. Treatment for the sufferer is to kill them.

McCajor Hall, quoted in Humphreys, 1999.

Questions

Below are some other examples of 'culture bound syndromes'. Which of the six categories listed in RLA 9 do you think Western psychiatrists would place them into?

1 'Susto' (Latin America): unhappiness and sickness caused because the soul has left the body after a frightening event.

2 'Rootwork' (southern USA): an explanation for illness based on witchcraft or voodoo.

3 'Hsieh-ping' (Taiwan): the individual is possessed briefly by an ancestral ghost who attempts to communicate with the family.

Real Life Application 10:

Koro

THY, a 32 year old Chinese cook, reported panic attacks and breathlessness, among other symptoms, at a psychiatric clinic. Previously he had tried to follow local healers' advice to regain his lost energy through drinking a boy's urine and eating a human placenta.

At the same time, THY started to notice his penis was shrinking into his abdomen, and this caused him to eat excessively to relieve an overwhelming hunger.

THY had had quite a difficult childhood, and then adult life, including excessive gambling, and strong sexual urges. He had not been married. Psychiatrists who have studied this condition see a fear of death as underlying all the other fears. There is often an excessive guilt and anxiety, particularly linked to real or imagined sexual excess.

Kiev, 1972.

Summary

• Koro is primarily excessive anxiety focused on the fear of the retraction of the penis into the abdomen, and thus death.

Questions

1 What is the key symptom of koro?

2 How might koro be labelled in Western society?

3 What are the physical symptoms of koro?

Differing diagnoses
Concerning the problem of whether mental illness is universal, the best known study is by Cooper *et al* (1972). They compared the diagnosis of schizophrenia by the New York State Psychiatric Institute and the Maudsley Hospital in London. There were differences in the diagnosis based on the same symptoms – the New York State Psychiatric Institute diagnosed twice as many people as schizophrenic as the Maudsley Hospital. At the Maudsley Hospital, the symptoms were diagnosed as other mental illnesses such as depression, mania, neurosis (anxiety disorders) or personality disorders.

Culture bound syndromes
Berry *et al* (1992) highlight three types of syndrome, as follows:
1 Absolute: the same symptoms and incidence rates are found around the world. Murphy (1976) argues that schizophrenia is found in many cultures under different names – for example, 'were' (Yoruba, Nigeria) and 'nuthkavihak' (Eskimo language).
2 Universal: the same symptoms are found around the world, but the incidence rates vary between cultures.
3 Culturally relative: the symptoms are unique to a particular culture – for example, the Hopi Indians' (USA) understanding of depression produces five states, none strictly conforming to the DSM categories (Manson *et al*, quoted in Stix, 1996):

• 'wa wan tu tu ya/wu ni wu' (worry sickness)
• 'ka ha la yi' (unhappiness)
• 'uu nung mo kiw ta' (heartbroken)
• 'ho nak tu tu ya' (drunken-like craziness with or without alcohol)
• 'qo vis ti' (disappointment and pouting).

Commentary

There are a number of illnesses that are distinctively Western based, but which appear in the main categories of the classification systems. These include chronic fatigue syndrome, eating disorders and Dissociative Identity Disorder (formerly Multiple Personality Disorder) (see also RLA 11).

Real Life Application 11:

Non-Western approaches to abnormal behaviour

Within Asia and Africa are traditions in how to deal with abnormal behaviour. In the main, psychology is not separate from spiritual matters. Also the individual with the problem is seen in the context of the family network, and treatment may focus on the whole family.

Africa

Traditionally a problem would be dealt with by the community's healer, who usually attributed the problem to a disruption in the person's relationship with the spirit world. This could be due to sorcery, the evil eye, the breaking of a taboo or the failure to perform required rituals. Treatment could include rituals, animal sacrifices, incantations or the use of special objects.

Asia

Traditional religions, like Buddhism, emphasize self-awareness, and thus separation from the world, by using meditation. The main aim is for individuals to deal with themselves guided by a professional. An emphasis on self-reflection can be seen in Naikan therapy (which attempts to remove self-centredness) and Morita therapy (both from Japan).

Summary

• Both Asia and Africa have their own traditional approaches to abnormal behaviour, which are different from the Western methods. The most important difference is that psychological problems are seen as linked to spiritual matters in these parts of the world.

Questions

1 Is psychology in the West separated from spiritual matters?

2 Does treating the whole family have a parallel in the Western treatments for abnormal behaviour?

3 What is the key difference between traditional approaches in Africa and Asia?

Bias in diagnosis

Another area of criticism is that there is bias in the diagnosis made. Psychiatrists are able to use the classification systems appropriately, but they are subjective in their diagnosis of different groups in society. The two main areas of bias relate to ethnicity and gender. The issue of ethnic bias can be summarized in the simple statement that psychiatrists are accused of being racist in their diagnosis. Fernando (1992), himself a psychiatrist, is most definite: 'Theory and practice are permeated by racist ideology' (see Table 2.4).

Boogra and Mallett (speaking on *All in the Mind*, 1996) report their study from Camberwell and Ealing comparing three groups: white, Afro-Caribbean and Asian. Whites were more likely to go to their GPs with psychological symptoms, while the Afro-Caribbeans saw hospital as the last resort. The Asian group saw the same symptoms not as a medical problem, but as stress. The Afro-Caribbeans were nearly twice as likely to be diagnosed as schizophrenic than the other two groups, based on the same symptoms.

There are also differences in the experience of hospital for sufferers of mental illness from different ethnic backgrounds. Takei *et al* (1998) followed up

Country of birth	Male	Female
Britain (base rate)	100	100
West Indies	136*	156*
Africa	121	129
Combined Afro-Caribbean	156*	185*
India	149*	123*
Pakistan	59*	191*
Combined Southern Asian	236*	325*

* = p0.01 compared to base rate

Rack, 1982.

Table 2.4: Index of first admissions data from selected studies in England and Wales in 1970/80s

| | Schizophrenia | | Non-schizophrenia | |
	White	Black	White	Black
Mean length of admission to psychiatric hospital (days)	124.4	272.8	72.9	67.7
Mean number of admissions	3.4	5.3	2.8	3.1

Table 2.5: Results from Takei et al (*1998*)

%	White	Black Caribbean	Black African	Black British	Asian/ Other
'Sectioned'	17	25	27	46	17
Schizophrenia	18	37	44	58	42

Table 2.6: Results from Bhui *et al* (1998)

81 patients who had been admitted to a psychiatric hospital with 'functional psychosis'. This diagnosis no longer exists, but it covers schizophrenia and affective disorders (see Table 2.5).

Fernando (1992) lists the conclusions from UK research to back up his assertion as follows:

- Over-diagnosis of schizophrenia among West Indian and Asian British. This means for the same symptoms, disproportionately more individuals from these groups were diagnosed as schizophrenic rather than any other illness.
- Excessive use of compulsory admission for West Indian British. Research in South London found that black patients with psychosis were three times more likely to be institutionalized compared to whites. 'Independent of psychiatric diagnosis and sociodemographic differences, black Africans and black Caribbean patients with psychosis in South London were more likely than white patients to have been detained under the Mental Health Act of 1983' (Davies *et al*, 1996, p. 533). Sayal (1990) found twice as many blacks were given compulsory admission than whites in the UK as a whole.
- Excessive transfer to locked wards of West Indian, African and Asian British. More individuals from these groups were put in locked wards when in a psychiatric hospital.
- Excessive admission of 'offender patients' among West Indian British. Individuals in this group were more likely to be put in prison than in hospital (1.4 times more in the South London study). Bhui *et al* (1998) investigated 277 men in Brixton Prison, London, on remand diagnosed as having 'potential mental illness'. The researchers looked at the diagnosis of schizophrenia and the recommendation of 'sectioning'. The figures, as percentages of that particular ethnic group, are shown in Table 2.6.
- Overuse of electro-convulsive therapy (ECT) among Afro-Caribbean and Asian British. Relatively greater use of this type of treatment among these groups.

It is important to emphasize that the differences are not due to differences in the prevalence of mental illness among the ethnic groups. It is, in the main, a product of the bias in the mental health system. This can be seen in the fact that such high rates of mental illness are not seen in the countries of origin.

Glyn Lewis (talking on *Medicine now*, 1994) outlined his research with 200 psychiatrists using four case histories – the only difference being whether the patients were described as white or Afro-Caribbean. A pattern appeared in the diagnosis given separately by the psychiatrists. For the Afro-Caribbean cases, more neuroleptic drugs were prescribed and more often criminal proceedings were recommended (that is, compulsory admission), but there was a less common diagnosis of schizophrenia. Lewis argues that psychiatrists are conscious of the criticism of being racist, but still respond in part to the stereotypes of particular ethnic groups.

In defence of British psychiatrists, since this report the Royal College of Psychiatrists has set up a Working Party on Ethnic Minority Issues, and a Special Interest Group in Trans-Cultural Psychiatry. But some would argue that while the vast majority of psychiatrists are white males the bias will continue.

Commentary

On a slightly different note, Irish people in Britain have the relatively highest rate of psychiatric hospitalization and are over-represented in most diagnostic criteria, including schizophrenia (Coppock and Hopton, 2000).

Similarly this argument links to the second type of bias, in the mental health system, against women. Lloyd (1991) noted that women made up 4% of the prison population, but 20% of the population of the Special Psychiatric Hospitals. Women who are aggressive, addicts or living rough are more likely to be diagnosed as anti-social personality disorder ('psychopathic') than men in the same situation.

Commentary

Historically, some mental illnesses have been seen as female-only disorders. For example, in the nineteenth century women who filed for divorce were viewed as mad. In fact, an English doctor Isaac Baker Brown advocated the performance of a clitoridectomy (the surgical removal of the clitoris) as a cure for such insanity. 'Women were believed to be more vulnerable to insanity than men, to experience it in specifically feminine ways, and to be differently affected by it in the conduct of their lives' (Showalter, 1986, quoted in Herman and Green, 1991, p. 16).

Challenges to the medical model

The biggest challenge to the medical model came in the 1960s with the growth of the anti-psychiatry movement. This questioned the assumptions of mental illness and criticized psychiatrists as controlling those who did not fit into society. Thomas Szasz entitled his book *The Myth of Mental Illness*. He believes that the mind is not an organ like the rest of the body, so it cannot be diseased as the rest of the body. Thus all abnormal behaviour is really a problem with living. So-called symptoms are based on an individual's communication ('communication symptoms') within a particular social and cultural context. Usually it is a subjective decision based on whether the observer believes the individual's claims to be, for example, the messiah.

Szasz saw the use of mental illness as a device to imprison non-conformists without trial. He quotes the case of 'Joe Skulski' (Szasz, 1974), who refused to move from his garage when property developers wanted to take over that area. When Skulski resisted the police, he was diagnosed as mentally ill and 'sectioned'.

Laing (1957), for example, saw mental illness as a cry of sanity in an insane world, which is suppressed by psychiatry.

Gorenstein (1984) points out that the term 'illness' leads to the 'authorization of care by a physician', and the 'assignment of a legal/ethical status that denies certain freedoms'.

However, DSM does distinguish between non-conformity (political, religious, sexual or conflict with society) and abnormal behaviour. Foucault (1967) has argued that the history of psychiatry is not a progression from cruel suppression to gentle concern as often portrayed, but the opposite, with increased government control in the twentieth century.

Thomas Szasz

Behavioural model

Though the medical model is dominant in Western psychiatry, there are other models of abnormal behaviour. The behavioural model does not talk about mental illness, but about maladjusted behaviour. For this model, any problem is simply maladjusted behaviour that has been learnt through classical and operant conditioning. Thus the aim of any therapy is to change this behaviour by learning new behaviour. Murdock and Barker (1989) see this as the 'direct modification of observable behaviour which has been identified as in need of change'. This can be behaviour that is both present or absent.

The main premise of this model is that all behaviour, except the most basic, is learned by the principles of the Learning Theory. Behaviour serves a function in the current context, and is maintained by events that precede or follow it. Thus maladjusted behaviour is learned by the same principles as adjusted behaviour, but it can be altered by applying the same principles of learning.

There are a number of types of maladjusted behaviour, as follows.

- Behaviour excess: a particular behaviour is shown too much – for example, a strong negative emotional reaction every time a particular object is seen. There can also be the opposite of this, which is that certain adjusted behaviours appear too little.

- Skills deficit: here a person lacks the skills to perform the necessary behaviour and this causes the maladjusted behaviour – for example, violent reactions to frustration because the individual does not have the social skills to negotiate.
- Behavioural deficit: the person is able to perform the behaviour, but fails to do so, or to do so enough.
- Behavioural conflicts: there is more than one consequence to the behaviour, which means that the person must choose between them leading to a behavioural deficit.

The basic principles of learning are classical and operant conditioning, which come primarily from work with animals. But, as far as Behaviourists are concerned, the principles of learning are the same for all species.

Classical conditioning

This is learning that takes place because of the association of two events together, and is based on the work of Ivan Pavlov, who discovered that ringing a bell every time his dogs were about to be fed led to the dogs learning that the bell meant food. Thus they produced saliva at the sound of the bell, which originally only occurred at the presence of the food. Learning is a reflexive process, in the main.

Applying this idea to maladjusted behaviour, like phobias, a phobic reaction to a specific object could be learnt because of an unpleasant association with that object, like a parent screaming in front of a child when that parent sees a spider. Watson and Rayner (1920) attempted to show this form of learning in a study with Albert B, known as 'Little Albert' (see Key Study 4, and Figure 2.3, page 28). However, in a similar study, English (1929) found no fear in a fourteen month old child after 50 pairings of a duck with a loud noise. Applying this principle to soldiers under fire, only some of them developed neurosis (Grinker and Spiegel, 1945).

Operant conditioning

This is learning based on what happens after the person does the behaviour. BF Skinner studied this at great length under the heading of Stimulus-Response (SR). If a behaviour is reinforced (rewarded) it will continue, and if it is punished, it will cease.

Thus any existing behaviour has been reinforced

KEY STUDY 4

Researchers: Watson and Rayner (1920)

Aim: To teach a child to be afraid of a white rat using the principles of classical conditioning.

Method: Using a 9 month old child called Albert, the researchers allowed him to play with a white rat. Initially there was no fear reaction. Then as he was playing with the rat, the researchers terrified the child with a loud noise. This was done a number of times. Here is how Watson describes the event from his notes (when Albert was 11 months old): 'Just as the right hand touched the rat, the bar was struck again. Again Albert jumped violently, fell forward and began to whimper.'

Results: Eventually Albert showed the fear reaction at the appearance of the rat. The effect was so powerful that Albert was afraid of a rabbit, a fur coat, cotton wool and a Santa Claus mask.

Conclusions: The researchers concluded that phobic reactions are merely conditioned emotional responses (CER) – that is, learnt.

---

for it to be existing. For example, individuals showing behaviours including hallucinations and thought disorders have been reinforced for such behaviour. People may only be paying the individual attention when the individual shows such behaviour.

Alternatively, individuals may not be showing appropriate behaviour because they have been punished in the past for doing so, and this behaviour ceased. For example, individuals who ate the normal amounts of food may have been criticized as being 'chubby' or 'fat', which leads to them not eating much in order to reduce their weight (eating disorders).

Reinforcement or punishment can come in any form. Reinforcement is always something desirable and punishment is based on something undesirable. Figure 2.4 lists the technical terms for operant conditioning.

'Little Albert': jargon terms

Unconditioned Stimulus (UCS): a stimulus that already produces a reaction e.g. loud noise.

Unconditioned Response (UCS): an already existing response eg crying at a loud noise.

Neutral stimulus: a stimulus that produces no response.

Conditioned Stimulus (CS): the learnt stimulus.

Conditioned Response (CR): the learnt response.

Before conditioning

Noise (UCS) ⟶ Crying (UCS)

White rat (neutral stimulus) ⟶ No response

During conditioning

White rat + Noise ⟶ Crying

(pairing together many times)

After conditioning

White rat (CS) ⟶ Crying (CR)

Extinction: reducing the frequency of the appearance of the CR by unpairing the UCS and the CS – e.g. the loud noise is not produced when the white rat is present.

Generalization: the spontaneous transferring of the CR to stimuli similar to the CS – e.g. Albert cried at the presence of white cotton wool.

Discrimination: learning to produce the CR only to the specific CS – e.g. learning fear reaction only to poisonous snakes.

Figure 2.3: Jargon terms for classical conditioning

Evaluation of behavioural model

It is important to Behaviourists that their principles are experimentally established, which is why many animal studies have been performed to establish the basic principles of learning.

This approach tends to focus on the now rather than seeking the actual past cause, which can be both an advantage and a disadvantage. Often individuals can be caught up in searching for the cause, and not concentrating on the now. On the other hand, it can be important to know the reason why a particular behaviour started or ceased in order to stop the future reoccurrence of the situation.

This model has been criticized for being mechanistic and seeing the individual as merely a product of stimulus-response. It tends to ignore the cognitive aspects of the individual. The model is also reductionist in that all problems can be reduced to a simple stimulus-response relationship.

Positive reinforcement: produces the desired behaviour by rewarding its appearance – e.g. the organisation Weight Watchers uses praise and encouragement for those who lose weight each week.

Negative reinforcement: increases the frequency of a desired behaviour by removing the stimulus that the individual wishes to avoid – e.g. an agoraphobic remains at home, thereby avoiding the anxiety of social situations and crowds.

Punishment: reduces an undesirable behaviour by using unpleasant consequences, either by removing something desirable (negative punishment) or adding something undesirable (positive punishment) – e.g. with the Token Economy System, tokens are used to change unacceptable behaviour to acceptable behaviour.

Behaviour shaping: teaches complex behaviour by reinforcement of individual stages of the behaviour – e.g. teaching patients who do not leave their beds by reinforcing getting up, then getting dressed, then making their beds.

Continuous reinforcement: reinforcement of the behaviour every time it appears.

Partial reinforcement: reinforcement of the behaviour on certain occasions – e.g. every fifth time it appears.

Figure 2.4: Technical terms for operant conditioning

Psychodynamic model

The psychodynamic model is based originally on the work of Sigmund Freud, though it has been developed by others since his death in the mid-twentieth century. However, there are a number of principles that most in the psychodynamic tradition would agree with (Thomas, 1996), as follows:

1 Unconscious motives largely determine human behaviour and consciousness. In other words, things are not what they seem. Freud outlined three parts to the mind:

- conscious
- pre-conscious
- unconscious.

The unconscious takes up most of the mind, but its contents are not available to the conscious mind. However, this does not stop it from determining behaviour, which is why the term 'dynamic unconscious' is used. So people do not know the 'real' reasons for their behaviour (that is, the unconscious ones), and all behaviour has an unconscious motive. The basis of any psychological problems must be in the unconscious. 'It follows that our ordinary accounts of ourselves and others (including psychologists) of what we

Sigmund Freud: the founder of psychoanalysis

do, what we feel and what happens to us are at best limited and most of the time are likely to be inaccurate' (Thomas, 1996, p. 286).

2 Our understanding of the world is distorted to avoid anxiety. The ego (the part of the personality that lives in both the conscious and unconscious mind) uses defence mechanisms to protect our conscious minds from psychological pain and anxiety. We are not aware that these processes are at work. The most common defence mechanisms are repression, denial and projection. Repression is where unpleasant memories are forced deep into the unconscious, and thereby are forgotten to the conscious mind. Denial involves the conscious belief that there is not a problem. Projection is the unconscious rejection of the anxiety on to another person, and usually to criticize it in them.

3 The early experiences of the child become the template for most of the adult personality and experiences. Freud placed great emphasis on the first five years of the child's life as it undergoes three stages of psychosexual development. In each case, the libidinal energy that gives pleasure lives in a different part of the body during the oral, anal and phallic stages of development. At each stage, how the child experiences the energy will affect their later life. For example, during the oral stage in the first year of life, the energy is cen-

tred around the mouth and the experience of feeding. Too much pleasure or too little can lead to oral fixations in later life (like smoking or biting the nails), and even the oral personality type. Fixations live in the unconscious mind. Table 2.7 gives examples of other fixations.

4 The means to discover what is happening in the unconscious is through psychoanalysis with the trained analyst, who can interpret the conscious signs and symbols of the unconscious motives and conflicts. 'Conflict' is a key term in psychodynamics because the whole personality is based on the conflict between the three parts of the personality, Freud believed. The id lives in the unconscious mind and is concerned with instant gratification, while the superego (partly in the conscious and unconscious mind) is an internalization of how the individual ought to behaviour ideally. This leaves the ego to maintain equilibrium between these two other parts of the personality (see Figure 2.5, page 30).

Oedipal complex

Within Freud's theory of a child's psychosexual development, the Oedipal complex, which boys face, is crucial. Freud's work on the female equivalent (Electra complex) is not well developed.

Around the age of four or five years old, boys start to have a sexual attraction for their mothers. However, the presence of the father who 'possesses' the mother is a rival. The boys come to fear the father,

	Fixation	Characteristics
Oral stage	'incorporative' – over-indulgence/ passive	cheerful, optimistic, self-centred, dependent, fluent, sociable
	'incorporative' – frustration/ deprived	greedy, envious, parasite, gluttonous, aggression, impatience
	'aggressive' – over-indulgence or frustration	cynical, sarcastic, scornful
Anal stage	expulsive	punctuality, orderliness, performing for others, giving
	retentive	obstinacy, miserly, wilful
Phallic stage		curiosity, exhibitionist, exploit others

Table 2.7: Personality characteristics based on fixations in psycho-sexual development

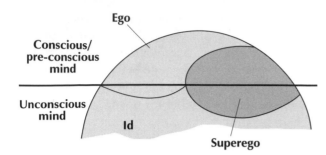

Figure 2.5: Theory of mind and personality

and castration anxiety develops. To resolve this anxiety, the child identifies with the father (that is, becomes like the father). The Oedipal conflict is predominately in the unconscious, so a child or an adult would have no memories if they were asked about it later in their lives. If this complex is not resolved, then many problems will exist in adulthood. For Freud, the most obvious was homosexuality.

The Oedipal complex is a difficult concept to prove or disprove. Freud supports his ideas with the case study of 'Little Hans' (1909). Hans was a five year old boy who developed a fear of being bitten by horses, and would not leave the house. Freud, after reading the details in letters from the father, interpreted the fear of being bitten as the conscious manifestation of the unconscious castration anxiety.

The whole episode had begun when Hans had seen a horse collapse in the street. Freud interpreted this as reminding Hans of the unconscious death wish he had for his father. Other researchers have suggested that this event classically conditioned a fear of horses. However, Bowlby (1973) argues that Hans' desire to be near his mother was a product of separation anxiety, not the Oedipal complex.

Evaluation of the psychodynamic model

Compared to the Behavioural model, the psychodynamic model is concerned with the whole personality and experiences. Individuals talk about their past and feelings rather than being conditioned to a new behaviour.

The main problems revolve around Freud's theory, which is difficult to test. Most of the concepts, like the dynamic unconscious or the Oedipus complex, have to be taken at face value because it is very difficult to prove their existence scientifically. Often this leads to a situation where whatever is said is seen as supporting the psychodynamic viewpoint. 'So if analysts see castration anxiety in their patients,

Freud is right; and if they fail to see it, they have "overlooked it" - and Freud is still right' (Tavris and Wade, 1995 p. 452).

Commentary

Fisher and Greenberg (1977) conclude, after an exhaustive study of the evidence on Freud's theory, that 'it is a complex structure consisting of many parts, some of which should be accepted, others rejected and the rest at least partially re-shaped'.

Cognitive model

This model places the emphasis on the thinking processes of the individual. Wessler (1986) sees this approach as 'a collection of assumptions about disturbance and a set of treatment interventions in which human cognitions are assigned a central role'. Thus problems are caused by maladjusted thinking. The psychologists usually most associated with this approach are Aaron Beck and Albert Ellis (see Chapter 3, page 47).

As with all the models, there are underlying assumptions to this approach, as follows:

1 The cognitive activity (that is, thoughts, memories and perceptions) of an individual affects his (or her) behaviour. The individual's interpretations give him a sense of understanding, prediction and control. Information is stored in schemata, which are cognitive structures that hold information. There may be schema for happy and pleasurable information, and for unhappy and unpleasurable information. Access to particular schema influence what information the individual brings to mind.

2 This cognitive activity can be monitored and altered.

3 Desired behaviour change may be produced through cognitive change.

4 Cognitive processes can be maladjusted in various ways.

In order to understand the individual with mental problems (the term 'mental illness' isn't used in this model), it is necessary to understand his (or her) cognitive processes. The individual is trying to make sense of the world, and is thinking about the meaning of his and others' behaviour. Thus 'automatic thoughts', attributions, expectations and self-efficacy are key concepts. 'Automatic thoughts' are those thoughts that occur without apparent reason, like an internal dialogue. For people with mental problems, the 'automatic thoughts' are usually negative.

Attribution is a general process of trying to explain behaviour – both our own and other people's – and events. It is the search for the cause of the event or the behaviour, which may be dispositional (that is, something about the person) or situational. For example, a person who often argues with people and consequently sees many relationships end, will make attributions about these events. Either the person will see him or herself as the cause (for example, 'I am an aggressive person'), or blame others (for example, 'Some people are unreasonable'). These attributions link to expectations. Sometimes it is more important what the person expects to happen than what actually does. Expecting a relationship to end in an argument can produce behaviour that makes this happen (a self-fulfilling prophecy).

Finally, attributions and expectations will be linked to self-efficacy – that is, beliefs about our own abilities to perform the task or achieve the goal.

Mischel (1979) argues that there are five variables that influence the response to a stimulus:

- competencies (the individual's unique set of abilities)
- encodings (how individuals categorize the world)
- expectancies
- values
- plans.

All of these ideas can be put together into attributional or explanatory styles. Stratton *et al* (1988) devised the Leeds Attributional Coding System for use in therapy. The explanatory style is based on three dimensions, as follows:

- Stable/unstable: concerned with whether the cause is the same in all situations (stable) or changes from situation to situation (unstable).
- Global/specific: whether the attribution is specific to one situation or explains all situations – for example, failure of a maths exam because student is poor at maths (specific) or poor at all subjects (global).
- Internal/external locus of control: an internal locus of control, the individual believes they control events, while with an external locus of control the individual feels that life controls them.

Normally if a person has success he or she makes an internal, stable and global attribution of the cause, and the opposite for failure. In other words, the attribution for passing an exam is own efforts/abilities (internal locus of control), which can be applied to all situations (stable/global). But failure of an exam could be a one-off (unstable/specific) because of an extremely difficult exam paper (external).

Figure 2.6 (see page 32) shows an example applied to losing a job. However, research has shown that depressed individuals apply the complete opposite explanatory styles. If they pass the exam, it is a one-off due to an easy exam paper, but failure is because the individual is not clever enough, for example. It is not clear whether this explanatory style difference is a cause or a product of depression.

Because the cognitive model is the basis of cognitive-behavioural therapy (CBT), much interest has been on errors or biases in the thinking processes that lead to mental problems. There are five particular errors to highlight, and these are given in Table 2.8 (see page 32).

Evaluation of cognitive model

The great strength of this model is that it concentrates on the thinking patterns of the individual now, rather than what happened in his or her childhood (psychodynamic model). However, this can mean that past events, which have a powerful influence on the individual, are neglected. This approach may succeed in changing the depressed person's thinking, but may not discover the underlying cause of the depression.

This model does depend on the individual being able to reflect on his or her own thinking. For severe problems, particularly with thought disorders, it is not possible to use this approach to help the person.

Humanistic model

This approach developed in the 1960s as an antithesis to the dominance of scientific psychology. This included the dominance of the medical model. There is an influence of anti-psychiatry in the humanistic model. This model is also known as the 'personal growth model' or the 'human potential model', and it can be linked to existential ideas and called the humanistic–existential model. This model obviously rejects the concept of mental illness, and talks about problems with living. Below are the main assumptions of this model.

1 Each individual is unique, so no general theory of behaviour and abnormality can be applied. It is

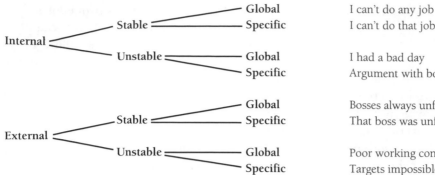

Figure 2.6: Attribution about losing a job

most important to understand the world from the individual's point of view – that is, his or her subjective reality. It is the here and now that matters.

2 The emphasis on human potential, which is limitless. People are innately good and they become faulty or bad through life experiences. It is fundamental for people to self-actualize – that is, to achieve their full potential. Everybody is capable of growth, which can include the spiritual aspects of life. It is the only approach to take account of this side of human experience. Many problems are caused because people are frustrated from self-actualizing by the demands of others.

3 Individuals are free to choose their behaviour, and therefore responsible for their actions. The freedom to choose is liberating, but the responsibility that goes with it makes some people avoid the choice. Yalom (1980) argues that many problems are due to defences against this autonomy that the individual uses. This could include displacing responsibility for his or her life on to other people, refusing to take decisions, behaving

impulsively without thought, compulsive behaviour or even acting 'mad' (that is, out of control). However, Fromm (1960) sees the escape from freedom by following political ideologies or religious belief systems, or letting fashion dictates the choices made. But the humanistic approach argues that there is no escape from freedom. In other words, 'to try to avoid the existential reality of choice is equally to choose' and 'guilt does not derive from transgressions against a particular moral code but from failing to live in an authentic way' (Stevens, 1996, p. 199).

4 Behaviour is actively directed at goals and is not passively a product of past experiences or learning. These goals relate to the purposes experienced by the individuals. Healthy individuals are self-aware of their motives in such choices.

5 The importance of 'authenticity'. This is facing the realities of life but, by doing so, it encourages personal growth. Life is about personal growth towards our full potential. The role of therapy with this model is to help the individual to

Error	Definition	Example from anxiety/ depression about work
Arbitrary inference	conclusion about event not supported by any evidence	feels not doing well at work, but everybody happy with their work
Selective abstraction	over-emphasis of one particular aspect of the situation	noticing how much praise another worker received from boss, and assume own work poor because not same level of praise
Personlization	taking responsibility for negative events that are not worker's fault	seeing general problems in office as his/her fault
Magnification and minimization	magnify minor events and minimize major events	everybody happy with work (minimize) except one person who does not have justifiable reasons (magnify)
Over-generalization	conclusion about worth based on limited evidence	feels failing as manager because not always praised by everybody

Table 2.8: Cognitive errors underlying maladaptive thinking

Carl Rogers

grow rather than having techniques to solve problems.

Carl Rogers

One of the main figures in the Humanistic movement is Carl Rogers. He emphasized the importance of looking at the person from that person's point of view. The primary motive of an individual is to maintain and improve oneself – that is, to realize one's potential (this is known as the actualizing tendency). If this is denied, there will be psychological problems. A person may perform certain behaviours in order to gain the positive regard of others, but this behaviour is in conflict with his or her need to actualize.

Many problems arise through 'incongruency'. This is a discrepancy between how we see ourselves (self-image) and how others see us. This is particularly the case when the motivation for behaviour, which is not actualizing, is conditions of worth – that is, doing certain things to be accepted by significant others. If an incongruent person is told he or she is successful, and it is inconsistent with that person's self-image, this can be threatening. Therefore, it is denied, which can cause maladjustment to living – that is, it produces a greater gap between reality and the self-image.

This situation can begin in childhood. The child learns to act in ways to gain approval (conditional positive worth), and these situations (conditions of worth) become part of the self. But, in time, this can lead to conflict with the actualizing tendency. The solution is unconditional positive regard, which allows the individual to actualize.

Model	Advantages	Disadvantages
Medical	diagnosis is basis to help find appropriate treatment	weakness with classification systems
	illness removes blame from individual	bias in diagnosis process
Behavioural	experimentally established principles	mechanistic and sees individuals as product of conditioning only
	deals with problems now, not in the past	reductionist assuming all behaviour can be reduced to stimulus-response
Psychodynamic	takes account of whole person	Freud's theory difficult to test
	individuals allowed to talk about past and feelings	many aspects of theory are seen as proved whatever happens
Cognitive	concentrates on individual's thinking patterns	no attempt to discover past causes of behaviour
	concentrates on thinking now	needs individual to be able to reflect on own behaviour, which not possible for severe problems
Humanistic	emphasizes freedom of individual to choose	assumes too much autonomy
	takes account of whole person, including spiritual aspects	does not help individuals with severe problems

Table 2.9: Comparison of the advantages and disadvantages of the main models of abnormality

Evaluation of humanistic model

This model is the only one that emphasizes the freedom of the individual to choose, and attempts to treat the whole person, including spiritual aspects. It is important to understand an individual's point of view rather than looking from the outside and commenting, as do the other approaches that we have already looked at.

However, this model assumes too much. Many people are not free to choose because of restrictions like lack of money or their position in society. These ideas appeal to young, rich and educated individuals in the West, who are unhappy with life, rather than having any major mental problems. It would not help individuals with psychosis.

Sayce (2000) argues that this approach can suggest that problems are the individual's own fault. She quotes the example of GROW, a twelve-step programme for those with mental illness, developed by the Church of Scientology. This programme states that mental illness is through learned habits of false thinking and disorganized living. The aim of the project is to change that thinking.

Table 2.9 (page 33) summarizes the strengths and weaknesses of each of the models that we have looked at in this chapter.

Essay questions

1 Discuss the assumptions of the medical model of abnormal behaviour.

2 Compare and contrast the psychodynamic and the behavioural models of abnormal behaviour.

3 Compare and contrast the cognitive and the humanistic models of abnormal behaviour.

3 Psychopathology

This chapter focuses on anxiety disorders, affective (mood) disorders, schizophrenia and eating disorders. In each case, details of the main symptoms will be included, along with the two most important explanations for that particular disorder. Real Life Applications that are considered are:

- RLA 12: Fears
- RLA 13: The pursuit of happiness
- RLA 14: Media and suicide
- RLA 15: A body to die for
- RLA 16: Telling the full story

Psychopathology is the technical term used to describe mental illness. Traditionally in psychopathology, the main distinction has been between neurosis and psychosis. Neurosis is seen as a problem that affects an individual, but he or she still has self-awareness and can live a relatively normal life, like a phobic. On the other hand, psychosis affects the whole personality and individual's life, like schizophrenia. Technically, the terms 'neurosis' and 'psychosis' are no longer included in the classification systems, but the main distinction between them remains. However, there are many exceptions to these distinctions – for example, an agoraphobic is afraid to leave his or her house and thus cannot live a normal life.

It is very difficult to establish the prevalence of mental illness because, in a number of cases, sufferers do not seek help or even recognize a problem. Estimates in Britain in the 1990s suggested that around 20% of adults were suffering from some form of mental illness (Meltzer *et al*, 1996). For neurotic disorders, the prevalence rate was calculated at 160 sufferers per 1000 of the population, and for psychosis the figure was 4 per 1000 (Chief Medical Officer, 1995). In the USA, lifetime prevalence for schizophrenia was estimated to be 1% to 2% of the population, major depression 4% to 7%, and anxiety disorders up to 20% (Robins *et al*, 1984).

A more recent survey of households in rural India found the following rates:

- anxiety – 2 per 1000 of the population
- schizophrenia – 3 per 1000
- depression – 74 per 1000 (Nandi *et al*, 2000).

The main conclusions from the many studies of the prevalence of mental illness is that sufferers are more widespread than is often thought.

Anxiety disorders

This is a group of illnesses based around anxiety. In the DSM classification system it includes Generalized Anxiety Disorder, Panic Disorder, Phobias, Obsessive-Compulsive Disorder and Post-Traumatic Stress Disorder as the main sub-categories.

Phobias

Many people have fears or anxieties about particular events or objects, and that is a normal part of life. But for it to be a phobia, it is the level of the emotional response that is different. A phobia is an extreme irrational fear (that is, severe reaction) focused on a specific event or object. The sufferer will then try to change his or her lifestyle to avoid the phobic object.

The phobic is more likely to be female, young (16–24 years old), less educated and unemployed. He or she is less likely to be married compared to non-phobics. The most common fears are insects, heights and enclosed or wide-open spaces. But there are also fears of eating in public and meeting new people.

Phobia is different from Panic Disorder because there is a focus for the fear reaction. Though the emotional reaction may be similar for both illnesses (see RLA 12, page 36).

Real Life Application 12:

Fears

Unusual phobias may be learned through disgust – a chocolate bar beside a dead relative leads to the fear of chocolate. Often the phobic object that cannot be seen is worse than the one that can be seen. This suggests a conditioning of cognitive processes rather than a conditioning of the fear.

Adapted from *All in the Mind*, 1992.

Approximately 40% of people suffer from a fear of the dentist, but for 5% of people it is a phobia. The fear may be so great that the sufferer is upset by toothpaste adverts or cannot walk along a street where a dentist is based. It is usually based on a previous bad experience.

You and Yours, 1993.

'Stage fright' is the number one fear in the USA.

Discover Magazine, 1997.

Donna Lampton has a fear of seeing buttons by themselves or in a box together – in particular, buttons that do not belong to anyone. Seeing a button on the pavement, for example, or on a bus seat makes her physically sick. Even talking about this is difficult. She remembers her grandmother having a tin of buttons, and, as a child, Donna had to find particular buttons for her grandmother from the tin.

Irrational Behaviour.

Summary

- As well as the common phobias such as snakes, spiders, heights and crowded places, there are many unusual ones.

Questions

1 How would the Behavioural model explain an unusual phobia?

2 What type of phobia is 'stage fright' related to?

3 Are there gender differences in the incidence of phobias?

Name	Fear	Incidence (of all phobias)
Agoraphobia	fear of leaving the house/ open spaces/crowded public places	up to 50%
Social	e.g. eating in public place	10%
Specific	e.g. spiders (arachnophobia)/ height (acrophobia)	up to 20%

Table 3.1: Most common phobias

Phobias and research

Research has tended to focus on the main groups of phobias (see Table 3.1). The main symptoms are listed in Table 3.2.

However, there are rare cases of phobias for almost any object or event. Listed below are some of the most unusual with their technical names.

- Bibliophobia: fear of books
- Pogonophobia: fear of beards
- Hyphnophobia: fear of sleep
- Apeirophobia: fear of infinity
- Scopophobia: fear of being stared at.

Commentary

Recent research has highlighted 'computer phobia' (Brosnan and Davidson, 1994), and 'tokophobia' (Hofberg and Brockington, 2000). The former can

Symptoms

Cognitive: thinking that the feared object or event will harm the individual. Often it is an exaggeration of a normally occurring event – e.g. the agoraphobic fears he or she will be attacked, even on an empty quiet street, if they leave the house.

Emotional: strong physiological reaction at the sight or thought of the feared item. The body produces a 'fight or flight' reaction, which is usually for emergency situations. It includes the heart beating faster, and adrenaline is released into the bloodstream.

Behavioural: the individual changes his or her life to avoid the feared situation.

Self-awareness: the individual is aware of the problem, and he or she changes behaviour to avoid the phobic item.

Misconception: that everybody has some fears, like spiders. The phobic reaction is much more intense and severe than a normal fear reaction. It is completely out of proportion to the danger – e.g. a household spider cannot harm the individual.

Table 3.2: Main symptoms of phobias

lead to the individual not even wanting to talk about computers, let alone use them. Tokophobia is the fear of childbirth.

Researchers interviewed 26 female sufferers in the West Midlands, of which five reported childhood sexual abuse and three traumatic rapes.

Agoraphobia

In a survey of 528 sufferers, Weekes (1973) found that 60% had not left their homes in more than ten years because of agoraphobia, while for 27% it was more than 20 years. Some 91% of the sufferers were female. There are degrees of this particular phobia varying from not leaving the house, to only leaving with someone else, or to not going to crowded public places.

Actress Stephanie Cole admits having suffered in the past. She talks about a fear, which included a dry mouth and trembling, caused by the exaggeration of what happens in the street – for example, louder noises or more threats (*Enemy Within*, 1995).

Social phobia

This can be a combination of a number different fears – for example:

- fear of being watched
- extreme self-consciousness
- fear of making a fool of one's self
- fear of social events.

The upshot is that sufferers do not like meeting new people, and they particularly do not like social events. This could go hand in hand with agoraphobia.

Some estimates place social phobia as high as 1 in 5 people suffering with some form, though only 2 in 100 people are actually diagnosed. It is possibly the third most common mental illness after depression and alcohol problems. Up to 50% of sufferers are disabled to a point of not facing others, and may even remain unemployed. This phobia begins in adolescence and is more common among men.

Charlotte Hadley went to an expensive restaurant for the first time and was ridiculed by her date for not knowing the correct cutlery to use. This led to a failure to form long-term relationships because she did not want to eat out. She had problems in the canteen at work with the fear of dropping food, using the wrong utensils or breaking a glass. This produced problems with swallowing and breathing, until she was only able to eat alone or with close family members (*The Guardian*, 1996).

Explanations of phobias

Explanations of phobias fall into three categories:

- evolutionary
- genetic
- other.

Evolutionary

This explanation sees the basic fears as an evolutionary benefit, but phobias are an excessive expression of this normal response. Any behaviour that helps individuals survive and pass their genes to the next generation develops through natural selection. So, for example, a fear of heights causes the individual to 'freeze', and thereby reduces the chances of falling.

Most primates show a fear of snake-like objects, which would suggest a 'preparedness' (Seligman, 1971) – that is, an evolutionary tendency to be afraid of what could be harmful. The preparedness hypothesis is based on three principles, as follows:

1 Certain stimuli (that is, related to survival) condition more easily than others.
2 The onset of the phobia is sudden.
3 The phobia is resistant to extinction.

Nesse and Williams (1996), who showed they had no fear of snakes, raised monkeys from birth in a lab. The monkeys were shown a video of a monkey making an alarm call at the sight of a snake. Subsequently, the lab monkeys showed fear of snakes. But this process did not work for flowers, though the same experiment was tried. See Key Study 5 (page 38) for an example of similar research with humans.

However, this explanation has a number of weaknesses, which means it cannot account for all phobias. For example, an evolutionary explanation does not apply with social phobias. There is no evolutionary benefit to avoiding eating in public or meeting new people.

The evolutionary model cannot explain why some individuals' fear response is excessive (that is, a phobia) and others' not. If there was an evolutionary basis, then most individuals would have similar responses.

Often the phobia of spiders or snakes is not a fear of harm but of having a panic attack (McNally and Steketee, 1985). Also, this model cannot explain the gender differences in phobias – that is, more women suffer from agoraphobia, and more men from social phobia. Nor does it explain the fact that spiders are kept as pets in South America, where there is little fear of them.

KEY STUDY 5

Researchers: Bennett-Levy and Marteau (1984)

Aim: To test the concept of preparedness, and in particular, what characteristics of animals humans are predisposed to fear.

Method: Some 64 participants rated the level of fearfulness of 29 small, harmless animals – e.g. rats, cockroaches, worms, frogs, rabbits. The participants used two questionnaires. There was a 3-point scale rating their fear of each animal (1 = not afraid to 3 = very afraid), and a 5-point scale for rating the nearness the participants would go to the animal (1 = enjoy picking it up to 5 = move further than 6 feet away). A further 49 participants rated the characteristics of the same animals. These participants used a questionnaire to measure four characteristics: ugliness, sliminess, speediness and how suddenly the animals appear to move.

Results: The ratings of fearfulness correlated significantly with the four characteristics of the animals. For example, there was a significant positive correlation of 0.82 between the ugliness of the animal and the level of fear.

Conclusions: The preparedness to fear certain animals is linked to the characteristics that are different from the human form rather than the animals themselves.

Genetic

Often phobias run in families, so it may be that they are inherited. In particular, agoraphobia has been studied in family studies. Harris *et al* (1983) found that where there was a first-degree relative (for example, mother, father, sibling) with agoraphobia, the risk of the illness was twice that of the control group (8.6% versus 4.2% of sufferers). Solyam *et al* (1974) found that 45% of agoraphobia sufferers had another family member who also suffered, compared to 19% for non-agoraphobic controls.

Even if the same phobia is not present in a family, there are often a number of different anxiety disorders in a particular family. Solyam *et al* (1974) found that 31% of phobics had a mother who suffered from some kind of phobia, while 55% had mothers and 24% had fathers with other anxiety disorders (like panic disorders).

But the problems common to a family could be learnt rather than inherited. According to the Social Learning Theory, people learn from observing others. So children could learn the phobic response from watching their parent's behaviour. However, Kleiner and Marshall (1987) noted that 84% of agoraphobics had family problems before the first attack (environmental stress).

Commentary

In animal studies, where inbreeding is possible, three genes related to anxiety have been isolated. But their influence is only a minor contributory factor to anxiety (Jonathan Flint speaking on *Science Now*, 1995).

Other explanations

Table 3.3 summarizes the other main explanations for phobias. Details of the main models (psychodynamic, behavioural and cognitive) can be found in Chapter 2 (see pages 28–30, 26–9 and 30–1).

Post-Traumatic Stress Disorder (PTSD)

This disorder was particularly noticed after the Vietnam War when participating US soldiers returned home. It has been estimated that 110,000 such veterans committed suicide as a result of their experi-

Psychodynamic	A blockage of unconscious impulses is transformed into neurotic anxiety through ego defence mechanisms
Behavioural	Learnt through classical conditioning – e.g. 'Little Albert' (see Key Study 4 in Chapter 2, page 27)
Physiological	Organic brain dysfunction (OBD – minor brain damage (Frampton, 1990)
Cognitive	Irrational thoughts after an unpleasant event – trapped in a lift becomes 'I could have suffocated', and thus a fear of using lifts
Feminist	Agoraphobia develops out of a need by women to repress their independence, which a male-controlled society does not appreciate (Fodor, 1974)

Table 3.3: Other explanations of phobias

ences and Post-Traumatic Stress Disorder (Focus, 1995).

PTSD was officially recognized in DSM in 1980. Before this recognition, it had been known under various names: 'soldier's heart' in the American Civil War, 'shellshock' (First World War), and 'combat neurosis' or 'battleground fatigue' (Second World War). Less pleasant names include 'cowardice' or 'lack of moral fibre'. Figure 3.1 gives a brief history of 'shellshock'.

The main focus of PTSD is that it develops following a psychologically distressing event, which lies outside common experience and that is an event distressing to most people. Thus the diagnosis is now much wider than just war veterans. DSM IV distinguishes three main variations of PTSD, as follows.

1 'Acute' – if the symptoms persist for less than three months.

2 'Chronic' – if the symptoms persist for longer than three months.

3 'Delayed onset' – if the symptoms do not appear until six months after the trauma.

'Acute Stress Disorder' is a different diagnosis for symptoms that occur within four weeks of the event, but last only a short period (between two days and four weeks). Some researchers have suggested that 'Gulf War Syndrome' may be a modern variation of PTSD combined with exposure to toxic chemicals (Hymans *et al*, 1996).

The risk of developing PTSD for the general population is 1%, but this increases with particular events. Shipwreck survivors have a 75% risk of developing it; bombing survivors, 50%; hi-jack survivors, 37%; rape and abuse victims, up to 50% risk. These are the primary victims – that is, the survivors of a traumatic event. There are also secondary and tertiary victims who have a risk of developing PTSD.

Secondary victims are families and those close to the victims (survivors or not), and it is estimated that they have an 80% risk. Tertiary victims are witnesses to the event (40% risk) and the emergency service staff/rescuers (15% risk). Freeman (1994) also adds 'peripheral victims' – that is, those who should have gone on the plane that crashes, for

Charles Myers (1915) coined the phrase 'shellshock' in the First World War to mean a physical shock from the bombing. Soon he realized that it was a mental, not a physical, problem. Sufferers often showed what was called 'hysterical conversion symptoms'. These are physical problems, like temporary paralysis of an arm, that have a psychological basis – for example, an apparent deaf man who responded only to the word 'bomb' even if whispered. His reaction was to hide underneath the bed. The main treatment initially for 'shellshock' was bed-rest.

The situation became worse when officers started to suffer. They were diagnosed as having 'neurosthania' to avoid the stigma of 'shellshock', and taken to separate hospitals.

Techniques to deal with 'shellshock' in the Second World War varied from 'narco-analysis' to 'deep sleep therapy'. The former involved the use of sodium amytal (the so-called 'truth drug') to make people talk about the trauma. The latter technique was long drug-induced periods of sleep (up to a month, sometimes).

After the Vietnam War came the use of the term 'Post-Traumatic Stress Disorder'. But the British military were sceptical initially.

Some individuals cannot escape the traumatic memories being reactivated and producing 'psychotic-like behaviour'. Morgan O'Connell talks about the case of Jimmy Johnson who killed two people during his 'flashbacks'. He was a British soldier in Northern Ireland.

The modern approach of the British army is short tours of duty to reduce the trauma. But the 'army culture' tends to hide the problems, and the use of alcohol (that is, 'having a drink with your mates') is seen as a more acceptable way to deal with trauma.
Shellshock, Wendy Holden, Channel 4 Books, 1998.

Figure 3.1: Effects of war

A survivor of a particular event, such as a bomb explosion, has a 50% per cent risk of developing Post-Traumatic Stress Disorder

example, but did not. They too can suffer from a form of PTSD.

The keys to the risk of PTSD are as follows:

- Whether the event is life-threatening or perceived as being so.
- The length of the event. Scott and Stradling (1994) suggest that PTSD can develop without a single traumatic event if there is prolonged exposure to stressors. They call this variation Prolonged-Duress Stress Disorder (PDSD).
- An individual's vulnerability to psychological problems. In a study of Israeli veterans of the 1982 war with Lebanon, Mikhliner and Solomon (1988) found that the difference between sufferers and non-sufferers of PTSD was the presence of a depressive attributional style – that is, the tendency to see negative events as their own fault and positive events as chance occurrences. Sufferers of PTSD tended to view the world this way. However, subsequent USA research has not found support for this difference.
- Whether an individual has an anxious disposition.
- Expression of emotions. Joseph *et al* (1997) found attitudes against expression of emotions correlated with higher symptom scores for PTSD with 37 survivors of the *Herald of Free Enterprise* disaster, five years after the event.
- Preparation for the event – that is, expected or

The 1950s and 60s pop icon Adam Faith was involved in a horrific car crash, which resulted in him suffering PTSD

unexpected, suddenness. Paton (1992) compared three groups of emergency service staff, and the level of PTSD among them afterwards. The groups were the police and medical workers after the *Piper Alpha* oil platform fire off the Scottish coast; firefighters and volunteer workers after an earthquake in Armenia; and volunteer nurses who went to work in the orphanages in Romania. The latter group suffered a much higher level of PTSD because they were not prepared for the level of suffering they found among the orphans.

- The level and type of support after the event. Table 3.4 (see page 41) give examples of different situations where PTSD have been found. But individuals can also suffer after relatively everyday events, like Adam Faith.

Pop star and actor Adam Faith experienced a bad car crash in the 1970s. It took him five months to recover physically. He still can't remember what happened five hours before the event and five months after it.

Following the crash, he experienced a change in personality. In particular he became obsessed with success. He was irritable, especially if he wasn't in control of a situation, and he took up 'macho' activities (for example, hang-gliding) to prove that he could overcome anything.

Faith became more emotional after the accident, which had an effect on his relationships; he also became oversensitive, particularly to criticism. It has taken him 20 years to recover from the experience. This, in part, is because PTSD was not recognized in this country for many years, and Faith was therefore unaware of the reasons he was experiencing such behavioural change (*Enemy Within*, 1995).

Symptoms of PTSD

The symptoms of PTSD can be divided into eight main groups, as follows:

1 Intrusive: sufferers cannot stop thinking about the event, though they want to do so. They experience flashbacks of the events, all thoughts lead to the event, and they have nightmares about it.

2 Avoidant: sufferers try to avoid any situation that could remind them of the trauma. But this goes with a numbness of response to anything, and a loss of interest in pleasure.

3 Denial: the denial of a problem or the effect of the trauma.

4 Feelings: sufferers feel increasing anxiety, pointlessness, along with shame, guilt or bitterness

Study	Sample	% lifetime prevalence of PTSD (DSM III criteria)
Centre for Disease Control (1989)	2490 USA army Vietnam war veterans	13.0
Kinzie *et al* (1986)	40 Cambodian adolescent refugees who immigrated to the USA	50.0
Saight (1989)	840 Lebanese children referred to Red Cross	27.5
Madakasira and O'Brien (1987)	116 tornado victims in South Carolina, USA	59.5
Kilpatrick *et al* (1987)	295 female crime victims	27.8
Weiseath (1989)	13 tortured Norwegian sailors in Libya for two months	58.3

Table 3.4: Selected studies to show different situations where PTSD has been found

about surviving. There is an overwhelming fear of the event happening again.

5 Behaviour: sufferers are unable to make decisions because of the above feelings, or they can be impulsive (which may be linked to anger and violence). There is irritability and an inability to concentrate.

6 Physical effects: the main physical effect is hyperactivity – that is, always prepared for another such emergency. Normal events become dangerous – for example, crossing the road after a car crash. This level of stress reaction can lead to physical illness, and/or increased smoking and drinking.

7 Change in value and beliefs: sufferers undergo major changes in their core values. This could include a loss of faith or purpose, or finding faith or purpose (for example, they survived because they had been 'chosen'). Not surprisingly, there are relationship problems.

8 Complicating factors: often PTSD is associated with panic attacks, depression and alcohol or drug abuse. One technique for measuring the symptoms of PTSD is a questionnaire known as the 'Impact of Event Scale' (IES). It contains a number of statements to which individuals rate their levels of agreement. Some examples from the IES include: 'I thought about it when I didn't mean to', 'I tried to remove it from my memory', 'I stayed away from reminders', 'I felt as if it wasn't real', and 'I am aware of unresolved feelings' (Paton, 1992).

Commentary

Traditionally, the view has been that sufferers of PTSD should be encouraged to relive the event. But recent research has shown that debriefing that focuses on re-experiencing the event can, in fact, increase anxiety and depression. Bisson *et al* (1997) worked with 133 burns patients. Half were given a debriefing for two hours two weeks after the event, and the other half received no help. Thirteen months later, sixteen of the debriefing group were diagnosed as having PTSD compared to four from the control group. Table 3.5 compares phobias and PTSD.

Children with PTSD

Brett *et al* (1988) list the following symptoms as being unique to children with PTSD.

- Repetitive play containing themes about traumatic events.

	Phobias	PTSD
Effect on life	limited to phobic object	whole life
Physical symptoms	panic reaction to phobic object only	hyperactivity; stress reaction most of time
Behavioural symptoms	avoid phobic object	avoid reminders of traumatic event
Cognitive symptoms	fearful thoughts about phobic object	intrusive thoughts
Awareness of self/problem	yes	usually

Table 3.5: Comparison of phobias and PTSD

- The loss of recently acquired developmental skills – for example, being unable to ride a bicycle after learning before the traumatic event.
- 'Omen formation': the false belief of being able to predict future untoward events.
- generalized fearfulness and separation anxiety when away from key adults.

Stallard et al (1998) studied PTSD among 119 children, aged between five and eighteen years, who had been in road accidents and compared them to 66 child with sports injuries. Some 41 (34.5%) of the first group were suffering from PTSD compared to two (3%) in the latter group. The key variables influencing the development of PTSD or not were the gender of the child (that is, girls suffered more), a previous experience of trauma in the last year before the road accident, and a subjective appraisal of a threat to life (that is, the child thought he/she would die). But the child's age and the type or severity of the injury were not significantly associated with the development of PTSD.

Explanations for Post-Traumatic Stress Disorder

Explanations for PTSD include the fact that it may be neurological or that it may be environmental (the diathesis-stress model). The text that follows examines these two explanations in more details.

Neurological

This explanation is based around the traumatic event causing a physical change in the individual, particularly to his or her brain chemistry. One such occurrence has been called 'noradrenergic burnout' by some researchers (van der Kolk et al, 1984). The reaction to the trauma leads to damage in the brain linked to the neurotransmitter noradrenaline. Noradrenaline is associated with many forms of behaviour and emotions, as well as wakefulness and arousal. The upshot is that the individual is more prone after the traumatic event to be startled and thus less resilient to minor stress. PTSD is partly, then, an over-reaction to everyday events.

Alternatively, it may be due to the large amount of adrenaline in the body during the stressful event. Adrenaline is released as part of the 'fight or flight syndrome', which is the body's emergency reaction to danger. Adrenaline also seems to be involved in laying down emotional memories. Thus the traumatic memories are strongly laid down in the memory, which means easy access to them at any trigger. Experiments with participants given beta-blockers (a drug that reduces adrenaline release) had less recall of an emotional film than a control group, while injecting rats with adrenaline after learning a new maze, increased their recall compared to the control groups. Also, an overproduction of the body's opioids, which are released in response to pain, could produce the feelings of numbness associated with PTSD.

Another possibility linked to neurology is based around the amygdala. This is part of the limbic system in the brain, and is associated with emotions and arousal. It seems that this part of the brain is in the 'on' position permanently, producing a high 'startle response' and an inability to recognize 'safety signals' that reduce the initial arousal. Thus the approach of a car, for example, triggers a 'startle response', but most people know that the car is not a danger if they are not in the way. Normally this reduces any initial arousal, but the PTSD sufferer still sees the approaching car as a danger.

However, Molloy et al (1983) found that USA Vietnam veterans showed the excessive arousal only to war-related stimuli. Veterans with PTSD were compared to veterans without and to a control group with other psychiatric disorders. All the groups were played various sounds, including war noises and everyday sounds. The heart rate was measured, and the participants could turn off the stimuli if it became too stressful. The PTSD sufferers showed increased heart rate, and were quicker to turn off war-stimuli than the other groups. No difference was found for the other types of stimuli.

Commentary

All the findings are correlations. So it is not clear whether the changes cause the PTSD or the PTSD caused the changes.

Diathesis-stress model

This model focuses on the environment and, in particular, environmental stress. Earlier trauma provides the basis for PTSD – that is, it produces a vulnerability.

Bremner et al (1993) found that PTSD was more prevalent in individuals who had childhood experiences of poverty, parental separation, abuse or catastrophes.

King et al (1999) analysed the data collected for over 1600 USA men and women who had seen combat in the Vietnam War. The researchers isolated the variables between those who suffered from PTSD and those who did not. It was found that an early history of trauma (that is, as a child) linked to additional life stresses at the current time to make certain individuals more vulnerable to PTSD. This was more so for men than for women.

Other research has found psychological risk factors that include anti-social behaviour as a child, depressive and/or neurotic behaviour before the trauma, and family instability and a history of psychopathology (O'Brien, 1998).

This vulnerability may also have a genetic element. Work with USA Vietnam veterans found that MZ (monozygotic – that is, identical) twins had a higher concordance rate for PTSD than DZ (dizygotic – that is, non-identical) twins (True *et al*, 1993). However, the genetic component had a greater influence on the higher level of arousal and anxiety, but not the re-experiencing of the event among PTSD sufferers.

Commentary

With reference to the Vietnam War, much of the research undertaken relates to the USA veterans, and none on the Vietnamese themselves who would have suffered as much, if not more. Banyard (2000) points out that it is a Western bias that has portrayed Vietnam as a USA tragedy, when over 95% of the casualties were Vietnamese. It was they who suffered massive bombing on their country. Much psychological research has a Western bias without realizing it.

Table 3.6 summarizes briefly the other main explanations for PTSD.

Affective (mood) disorders

It has been estimated that around 11 million people in Britain will suffer from a mood disorder at some stage in their lives. Usually it will be a short episode. The vast majority of sufferers will not seek professional help. For example, 1 in 20 people may suffer

Behavioural	Extreme case of classically conditioned fear; everything that happened during the traumatic event becomes associated with unpleasant emotions
Social construction	Construction of USA society in 1970s and 80s – i.e. USA Vietnam veterans only received help if diagnosed with 'real problem' (medically defined)
Psychodynamic	Trauma reactivates previously unresolved psychological conflict hidden in the unconscious mind

Table 3.6: Other main explanations for PTSD

from some form of depression, but 3 in 1000 will seek help from a psychiatrist.

Mood disorders are, in the main, depression or mania, and a combination of both. The sufferer's whole life is affected by this disorder.

Both ICD 10 and DSM IV distinguish between 'episodes' and 'disorder'. A manic or depressive episode is relatively short lived, whereas Bipolar Disorder or Depressive Disorder are longer term or recurrent. There is also the category of persistent mood states for cases that are unchanging. These can be either cyclothymia (manic) or dysthymia (depressive).

Depression

In the past, the distinction was made between

1 I feel as if I am slowed down:
   a nearly all the time
   b very often
   c sometimes
   d not at all

2 I still enjoy things I used to enjoy:
   a definitely as much
   b not quite as much
   c only a little
   d hardly at all

3 I feel cheerful:
   a not at all
   b not often
   c sometimes
   d most of the time

4 I have lost interest in my appearance:
   a definitely
   b I don't care as much as I should
   c I may not take quite as much care
   d I take just as much care as ever

5 I can laugh and see the funny side of things:
   a as much as I always could
   b not quite as much now
   c definitely not so much now
   d not at all

Scoring	Q1	Q2	Q3	Q4	Q5
a	3	0	3	3	0
b	2	1	2	2	1
c	1	2	1	1	2
d	0	3	0	0	3

Higher score = greater likelihood of depression. This is only a sample of items, so it is not an accurate measure of depression

Zigmond and Smith, 1983; reprinted in *The Observer Magazine*, 1992.

Figure 3.2: Items from hospital depression scale

Major Depressive Disorder

Major Depressive Disorder is diagnosed, in the main, based on evidence of at least five of the following:

- poor or increased appetite (at least 1 lb per week change in weight)
- sleep difficulty or sleeping too much
- loss of energy
- psychomotor agitation (e.g. nervous movement of limbs)
- loss of interest in pleasurable activities
- feelings of self-reproach
- inability to concentrate
- suicidal interests.

Minor Depressive Disorder

Minor Depressive Disorder is based on evidence of at least five of the following:

- crying often or continuously
- pessimistic thoughts
- brooding about past unpleasantness
- preoccupation with feelings of inadequacy
- feeling resentful, irritable and/or angry
- needing reassurance
- feeling sorry for self
- physical complaints without physical cause.

Figure 3.3: Diagnostic criteria for depressive disorders

Country	% of overall population
Lebanon	19.0
France	16.4
Italy	12.4
New Zealand	11.6
Canada	9.6
Germany	9.2
USA	5.2
South Korea	2.9
Taiwan	1.9

Economist, 1998.

Table 3.7: Lifetime prevalence rates for major depression around the world

reactive or neurotic depression, and endogenus depression. The former type (also known as exogenous depression) was linked to a specific event and the sufferer experienced more conscious guilt and fatigue, while endogenus depression had no obvious event as the trigger, and the sufferer showed stooped posture, slow speech and suicidal wishes. Usually depression is measured by a self-rating questionnaire (like the example in Figure 3.2, page 43).

Because of the problems of distinguishing the differences in diagnosis, ICD 10 and DSM IV now use Major Depressive Disorder (MDD), Minor Depressive Disorder or Dysthymic Disorder. MDD is severe and short term, while Dysthymic Disorder is less severe and lasts longer (that is, two years with less than two months' break). Figure 3.3 gives the full diagnostic criteria for minor and major depressive disorders.

Depression is by far the most common of all mental illnesses suffered. In the UK, 1 in 50 people are currently suffering from Major Depressive Disorder, while 1 in 5 will suffer at some stage in their lives. The rates vary around the world (see Table 3.7). The majority of sufferers (4 out of 5) of MDD do seek help. For other forms of depression, help is sought less often.

Because of the hidden nature of much of the

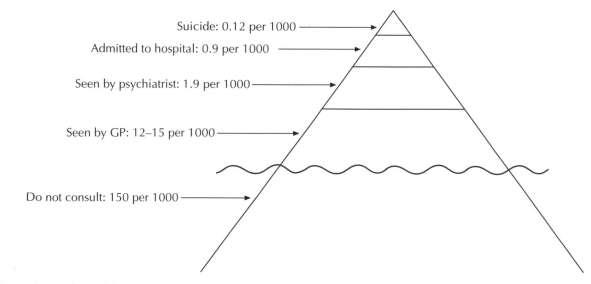

Figure 3.4: 'Iceberg of depression' (Watts, 1989)

depression that is suffered, there is what is called an 'iceberg of depression' (see, Figure 3.4, page 44).

Symptoms of depression

The symptoms of depression can be grouped under four main headings, as outlined below. (The difference between minor or major depression will be the intensity of the symptoms.)

- Cognitive: sufferers have a distinctive pattern in their thinking processes. There is an inability to concentrate with a poor memory. Most thoughts are negative, even suicidal. Sufferers tend to have low self-esteem, and have negative thoughts about themselves and life.

- Behavioural: sufferers shows a change in their behaviour, which includes a change in their eating and sleeping patterns. It can be either an increase or a decrease. So, for example, individuals may sleep for excessive periods, or have problems sleeping. They lose interest in caring for themselves (and others), and there may be suicide attempts (parasuicide). Responses to other people may become shallow and mechanical.

- Emotional: the strongest emotion is obviously sadness, accompanied by apathy. Sufferers may also be irritable. Another symptom is anhedonia, which is the loss of the ability to feel pleasure from normal pleasurable events, and so consequently the individual does not partake in those activities any more (see RLA 13).

- Physical: depression can also manifest itself in physical symptoms like general aches and pains, and loss of energy. For those not eating, there is a noticeable loss of weight. For women, there may be menstrual changes.

Real Life Application 13:

The pursuit of happiness

Lizzie Gardiner has suffered for many years, on and off, with depression. One of the worst, but often overlooked, symptoms is anhedonia. The sufferer has little or no ability to feel pleasure from normally pleasurable experiences. In other words, there are no longer any positive emotions.
Lizzie talks of depression as 'an illness which other people can't see', and those who have never experienced it are not always sympathetic. They often accuse the sufferers of depression of becoming a 'victim of their own misery', and not even trying to help themselves. But it's not possible to 'drop' the depression and 'get a grip'.

Adapted from 'The pursuit of happiness',
The Guardian, 4 April 2000.

Summary

- Anhedonia is often the worst symptom of depression because nothing gives the sufferer pleasure any more.

Questions

1 What type of symptom (that is, cognitive, behavioural, physical or emotional) is anhedonia?

2 What cognitive bias stops sufferers of depression from 'getting a grip'?

3 When non-sufferers of depression accuse sufferers of becoming 'victims of their own misery', what kind of attribution is being made?

Differences in depression

The differences in depression can be seen as relating to gender and age.

- Gender: research suggests that around twice as many women than men are diagnosed as depressed, even standardizing for age and diagnostic differences. Nolen-Hoeksema (1990) notices this difference only, however, in the developed countries. Research has failed to find a biological explanation for these differences. The argument that it is hormonal for women has no support. Cochrane (1995) places great emphasis on the acceptable way in society of coping with stress for men and women in Western countries. For men, they are more likely to cope with stress and life events by substance abuse (for example, alcoholism), and there is a noticeably higher rate of alcohol addiction among men than women. For women, the acceptable way is self-harm and depression. This argument is supported by research with the Amish community in USA. Within the community, alcohol is not permitted and depression rates are the same for both men and women.

- Age: it is often assumed that children and teenagers do not suffer from depression. But a study at Newcastle Psychiatric Unit of 300 children aged between nine and sixteen years old found that one-third had chronic depression (reported in *RCN Nursing Update*, 1996). Illman (1997) reports a survey of first-year university students in this country where 61% reported feeling depressed sometimes and 12% felt suicidal (with 1% attempting it). Similarly, depression among the elderly often goes unnoticed or is ignored. Copeland *et al* (1987) found in a Liverpool study that 11.3% of the residents at a community home (aged 65+) were depressed. Often the symptoms are manifest as physical illness.

Suicide and parasuicide

Approximately 4000 people in the UK each year commit suicide. In fact, one of the government's 'Health of the nation' targets is to reduce this figure

Real Life Application 14:

Media and suicide

Researchers have investigated whether media attention on suicide, like a fictional story, influences the actual rates of suicide. In particular, the BBC hospital drama *Casualty* often has cases of parasuicide.

In February 1997, one episode contained an attempted self-poisoning with anti-freeze. Veysey *et al* (1999) found that the average cases of the same type of parasuicide increased to six per month, in the hospitals studied, from a baseline of two per month before the programme.

In another episode of *Casualty*, there was a case of a paracetamol overdose. Hawton *et al* (1999) studied 49 UK Accident and Emergency Departments for general overdoses and, specifically, paracetamol overdoses. The average increase, in the first week after the programme, was 17% for all overdoses and 19% for paracetamol cases. Over the month after the programme, the average increases settled at 7% and 12% respectively. The researchers also interviewed as many survivors as possible, and about 25% reported having watched the programme.

Summary

- Fictional stories involving suicide can lead to an actual increase in parasuicide.

Questions

1 What is parasuicide?

2 Is there a theory of behaviour that could explain the imitation of behaviour from the television?

3 Why was the average increase for overdoses over the month of the study by Hawton *et al* less than the first week?

by 20% by 2010. This rate can be influenced by soap operas showing suicide (see RLA 14).

The term 'parasuicide' includes attempts at suicide as well as those that succeed. Usually there is a success rate of 1 per 25 attempts. The vast majority of attempts are by women, whereas the attempts by men tend to succeed. This is partly because the methods used by men and women differ. Men use more violent means, like shooting or hanging, whereas women may use overdoses or self-poisoning.

The Samaritans distinguish three groups of parasuicides:

- those who want to die
- those who don't want to live
- those who want to go to sleep.

Over 60% of cases had seen a GP in the last month. The vast majority of parasuicides will be suffering from depression. Beck (1976) also adds a small number of attempts to show others the seriousness of the problems, and to manipulate their behaviour in some way.

There are a number of myths about suicide, which are not supported by the statistics (see Table 3.8, page 47), and certain groups are higher risk (see Table 3.9, page 47).

Commentary

Suicide by young men doubled in the 1990s to become the second most common cause of death after road accidents for that age group. There are changes in society that could explain the increase, as outlined below (*All in the Mind*, 1999).

Myth	Truth
Young women are highest risk	Young men are three times more likely, and this increases with age
Parasuicide occurs at the depth of despair	It occurs often when misery is lifting, and there may be a minor setback
Those who talk about it never do it	8 out of 10 cases give warning beforehand in some form
Only people of certain social class commit suicide	Equally prevalent in all social classes

Table 3.8: Myths and facts about suicide

- The phenomenon of social isolation – that is, more men moving away from home to get jobs.
- 'Information glut' of what could go wrong in the future, like environmental catastrophes.
- 'Male narcissism': increasing pressure for men to worry about their appearance.
- Lack of outlets for young men when they need help.

Explanations of depression

Explanations of depression include the fact that it may be cognitive (that is, it focuses on the thoughts of the individual) or that it may be environmental

- Male
- 35–44 age group
- Living alone
- Unskilled
- Unemployed
- Those with means to kill – e.g. farmers, vets, pharmacists
- Homelessness
- Psychiatric illness
- Previous attempts
- Highest risk at beginning of treatment – e.g. anti-depressants can take up to three weeks to have an effect
- Recent loss event and/or unresolved stress
- Among elderly: highest risk are those with physical and mental health problems, and isolated
- Among teenagers: history of abuse; substance abuse; family turmoil; break-up of close relationship; illness; previous attempts; homosexuality

Borton, 1976

Table 3.9: High risk groups and risk factors for suicide

(the diathesis-stress model). The text that follows examines these two explanations in more details.

Cognitive explanation
This explanation focuses on the thoughts of individuals, particularly about themselves, about events that happen to them in their lives, and about the future. Beck calls this the 'cognitive triad'.

Lewinsohn *et al* (1981) give the example of over-generalizing from failures and focusing on negative characteristics – thus magnifying the importance of minor negative events. Schemata are ways of storing information in the brain. The cognitive process is shown in Figure in 3.5.

Another everyday example could be the ending of a relationship. Most people feel low about this event, but because of the negative thoughts, certain individuals become depressed. The negative thoughts could be, for example, 'She knew me and rejected me; there must be something seriously wrong with me' or 'I'm too old to find another person; I'll be lonely for the rest of my life'. These negative thoughts become 'negative automatic thoughts' – that is, individuals base their behaviour on them, and so they become depressed.

Similarly, Ellis (1962) argued that there are common irrational beliefs that underlie much depression, and sufferers have based their lives on these beliefs – for example, 'I must be successful, competent and achieving in everything I do if I am to consider myself worthwhile' or 'It's easier to avoid facing many of life's difficulties and responsibilities than to face them'.

Williams (1992) suggests there are certain factors in childhood that lead to the depressive schema, such as:

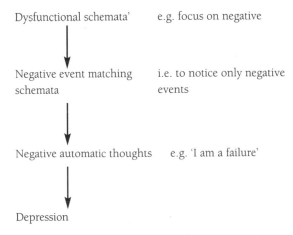

Figure 3.5: Cognitive processes in depression

- the loss of a close relative
- expectation of loss (real or imagined) – for example, after a long illness a parent either dies or gets better
- events that lower the child's self-esteem, like poor school performance
- background factors including depression in close family member(s), severe parental punishment, or isolation from other children.

The cognitive explanation of depression also takes into account the expectations of individuals themselves, their perception of events and the later recall of those events.

Commentary

Mark Williams (speaking on *Science Now*, 1995) reports evidence of a 'mnemonic interlock' among depressed and suicidal individuals. The way information is stored in their memories is such that they tend to remember only general positive events (for example, wedding days) rather than specific ones (for example, their own wedding day). This memory is biased towards negative memories because recall is 'stuck' at the level of general memories. This shows itself in a tendency to overgeneralize about events – for example, 'always' or 'never'. Overall the depressed person is showing cognitive biases in the way he or she views, understands and experiences the world.

This 'explanatory style', as it could be called, has been linked to learned helplessness (Seligman, 1975), which has become adapted into the 'hopelessness theory of depression'. Learned helplessness is the situation where the individual feels there is no hope and so is unable to change anything that is within his or her control. The original research was based on experiments with dogs (Overmeier and Seligman, 1967), but the phenomena has been shown experimentally with humans (see Key Study 6). Figure 3.6 shows an example after failing an exam.

The symptoms of learned helplessness can be seen as parallel to the behaviour of a depressed person – for example:

- lowered initiation of voluntary responses – that is, rarely makes an active move
- negative 'cognitive set' – that is, negative overall perception of the world
- the behaviour persists over time
- there are lowered levels of aggression
- there is a loss of appetite

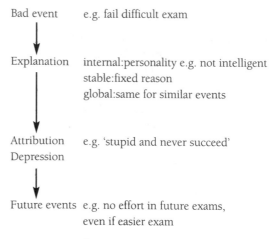

Figure 3.6: Failing an exam and learned helplessness

KEY STUDY 6

Researchers: Hiroto (1974)

Aim: To show the behaviour of learned helplessness in humans in certain situations.

Method: The participants were divided into three groups, and each group experienced two situations. The first situation was predicted to influence behaviour in the second situation. In the first situation, the participants were placed in a room with either a loud noise that could not be avoided, a loud noise that could be avoided or no noise at all (control group).

Results: Depending on the first situation, participants showed different behaviour in the second situation.

Situation 1	Situation 2	Participant's reaction to situation 2
inescapable noise	→ escapable →	passive:no attempt to escape (learned helplessness)
escapable noise	→ escapable →	attempt to escape
no noise (control)	→ escapable →	attempt to escape

Conclusions: Iindividuals who are in a situation that is inescapable develop learned helplessness, which means that they do not try to escape in the future, even when the opportunity is available. If this is the case, then those with depression cannot simply 'pull themselves together'.

- there are physiological changes – such as lower levels of arousal.

The cognitive explanation of depression does have its critics. The explanation does not distinguish between the different types of depression, but gives the same basic explanation. It cannot account for the physical symptoms that often accompany depression. Also it is not clear whether the cognitive biases are a product of depression as much as the cause.

Diathesis-stress model

This explanation focuses on the environment and life events experienced by the individual. Together a combination of these factors provide a vulnerability to depression. One negative life event or environmental variable may cause mild short-term depression, but it is a series of factors that work together to produce the long-term more serious depression.

A whole series of negative life events and environmental factors have been studied. Brown and Harris (1978) undertook a survey of 539 women in Camberwell, south London. Their aim was to distinguish between women who were depressed and those who were not, and to isolate the differences between both groups. The researchers found that 61% of those depressed had experienced stressful life events in the last nine months, compared to 25% of the non-depressed group. Altogether the researchers found a combination of factors that produced a vulnerability to depression: having three or more children living at home; the loss of the women's mother before aged 11; a low level of self-esteem among the women; and lack of a close confidant or friend (37% of the sample without a close friend became depressed compared to 10% of those with). Brown

and Harris combined the factors into a model (see Figure 3.7).

Commentary

The research sees all the factors as having an equal effect on each person. For example, having three children is not such a problem if there are childcare facilities available.

Leff *et al* (1970) identified stressors preceding the onset of severe depression. For example, 20% of sufferers had experienced the recent death of a close relative, 30% serious physical illness, 45% a job or house change, 47% marital disruption (that is, divorce or separation), and 75% an 'identity threat' (for example, failure to meet the demands of their sex role).

Studies have also found the importance of early experiences in setting the vulnerability to depression. Sadowski *et al* (1999) based their research upon the 'Newcastle Thousand Family Study', which follows 1142 children born between 1 May and 30 June 1947. The researchers found a clear correlation between family disadvantage in the first five years of life, and mental health problems at age 33.

Family disadvantage includes divorce or separation of the parents, long-term parental illness, poor physical care of the child and the home, overcrowding and poor mothering. Those individuals who had multiple disadvantages were four times more likely to suffer from depression. For women, the development of depression was also particularly linked to the quality of parenting in their early lives.

In a similar vein, Cheasty, Clare and Collins (1998) found an association between childhood sexual abuse and adult depression in women in a Dublin sample. Some 67% of those depressed reported abuse compared to 33% of the group not depressed. The severity of the abuse was also crucial. Some 56% of those 'touched' as a child became depressed compared to all the women who had experienced sexual intercourse or anal intercourse as a child. The researchers also showed a subsequent combination of problems for those abused: they were more likely to have housing problems, problems with their children at school and sexual problems themselves.

Maciejowski *et al* (2000), in their USA study, found a cycle where stressful life events trigger depression in individuals with low self-efficacy (an individual's belief in his or her ability to achieve certain goals), which then makes them vulnerable to

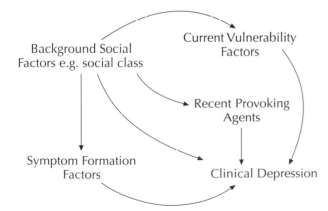

Figure 3.7: Brown and Harris's model of vulnerability to depression

Genetic	Limited evidence of depression common in families; studies with Amish community suggest possible link to chromosome 11 defect
Biochemical	Lack of certain neurochemicals, in particularly serotonin; or elevated levels of stress-related chemicals in the blood – e.g. cortisol. The symptoms of depression have been found among sufferers of Cushing's syndrome, which is caused by excessive cortisol in the body
Psychodynamic	Loss is a trigger for depression because it brings back memories of the childhood loss of parental affection.
Viral	Limited evidence of Borna disease (a viral inflammation of the brain) in depressed humans, and rabbits who are sluggish (Amsterdam *et al*, 1985).
Neuroanatomy	Various suggestions, with limited support, include relatively ineffective left frontal cortex, and differences in blood flow to areas of brain linked to emotions.

Table 3.10: Other main explanations of depression

subsequent negative life events. This undermines their self-efficacy, and increases the depression and the further vulnerability.

Table 3.10 summarizes briefly the other main explanations for depression.

Other types of depression

Other types of depression include Seasonal Affective Disorder and post-natal depression. Each of these is covered below.

Seasonal Affective Disorder (SAD)

SAD is estimated to affect half a million people in the UK between September/November and March/July. It is a specific form of depression that occurs only in the winter months. There is a definite correlation between the amount of daylight and the reporting of the symptoms of SAD. For example, in one survey in northern USA, in April (average daylight 780 minutes) only 30% reported the symptoms compared to 98% in January (average daylight 580 minutes). The symptoms of SAD include:

* sleep problems – that is, falling asleep early in the evening or waking late in the morning
* lethargy and energy loss
* depression
* irritability

Sad	Classic depression
Onset autumn; relief summer	onset/relief any time
sleep more	sleep problems
eat more	appetite change
mood influenced by daylight	no influence

Table 3.11: Comparison of SAD and classic depression

* desire to avoid social contact
* craving for carbohydrate and sweet foods, with consequent weight gain
* anxiety
* loss of libido.

SAD is different to classic depression, though there are similarities (see Table 3.11).

The cause of SAD has been linked to living in northern latitudes with long periods of darkness throughout the year. This is linked to the abnormal production of the hormone melatonin in many SAD sufferers (Lewy *et al*, 1987). Support comes from the fact that SAD sufferers who use 'light therapy' (that is, intense light equivalent to summer sunlight) each day in the winter show a reduction in symptoms.

Another suggestion is a link to hibernation in the evolutionary past. Recently, Teodor Postolache has argued that SAD sufferers have a more acute sense of smell, and this makes them more aware of seasonal changes. Similar acuity in smell among hamsters prepares them for hibernation. Hamsters with olfactory bulbs surgically removed do not prepare for hibernation. This theory about SAD has limited support (Pendick, 2000).

Post-natal depression

Another specific type of depression is post-natal. This occurs between three months to one year after the birth of the child. It is estimated to affect between 10% and 25% of women. It is different from a short-lived slump after the birth. The symptoms include:

* problems with sleep
* irritability
* tension and panic
* confused and obsessional thinking
* feelings of isolation, sadness and morbidity
* feelings of anxiety, guilt and unworthiness.

Marshall (1993) notes a number of contributory factors, including: high expectations about the birth and the child; fear of failure as a mother; ignorance about the reality of babies; changing relationships with others, and grief over loss of freedom (and work). Paradice (1996) discovered, in detailed interviews, that many new mothers admitted missing old lifestyles and old body images, but were unable to tell anyone because it was socially unacceptable.

It is important to distinguish post-natal depression from the rare condition of 'puerperal psychosis', which affects approximately 1 in 1000 mothers in the UK. With this condition, the symptoms are hallucinations and delusions, and negative feelings towards the baby. This view can include the belief that the baby was replaced in the hospital by another exactly the same. In an extreme form, the mother may kill the baby and/or herself. But most sufferers show manic symptoms before the birth of the child.

Mania/Bipolar Disorder

Mania is the complete opposite to depression, but it is not a pleasant 'high'. This is a misconception. Often there is a sense of intense euphoria or elation, and the individual needs little sleep or food. But there are many negative symptoms, such as those listed below, that make the experience of mania far from pleasant. Those who suffer:

- have fantastic ideas that are pursued with poor judgement, often involving loss of large amounts of money
- have extreme over-confidence, which leads to anger and irritation when others do not agree
- are easily distracted
- have hallucinations and persecutory delusions in some cases
- have an inability to remain still or quiet.

The sufferer's whole life is affected because he (or she) believes his delusions of invulnerability or his perceived inability to achieve. Manic depression (Bipolar Disorder, as it is now called) involves the alternation between the two extremes of mania and depression, with only a brief period of 'normal' behaviour in between. Each sufferer has an individual pattern, but this is the general cycle, as listed below:

- days 0–23: depression
- day 24: switch
- days 25–29: manic
- days 30 and 31: hypermanic
- days 32–45: depression
- day 46: switch
- days 47–53 manic.

Composer Robert Schumann: identified as almost certainly having Bipolar Disorder (formerly known as manic depression)

The rate of parasuicide can be high among this group of sufferers simply because of the intensity of the two extremes of emotions. Rihmer *et al* (1990) calculated that 47 of 100 suicides in Hungary were Bipolar Disorder sufferers.

There have been many famous sufferers, including artists and writers. Based on studies of biographies, Jamison (1995) feels that sufferers included the poets Coleridge and Keats, authors James Joyce and Virginia Woolf, and the composers Mahler and Handel. In fact, Jamison believes that nearly 40% of British poets born between 1705 and 1805 were sufferers. Among creative individuals generally, the rate of Bipolar Disorder is 10 to 20 times greater than the average population, and the suicide rate 18 times greater.

Many creative individuals are also extremely productive during their manic phases. Jamison (1995) charts the life of the composer Robert Schumann and the amount of works produced (see Table 3.12, page 52).

Explanations of Bipolar Disorder

There is evidence to suggest that Bipolar Disorder is genetic (that is, it is inherited). First-degree relatives (parents, siblings, children) of sufferers have up to a 20% risk of developing the illness compared to a 2% risk for the general population. Jamison (1995) researched the family tree of the poet Alfred, Lord

Year	Number of pieces composed	Comment
1833	2	suicide attempt
1840	24	manic
1844	0	severe depression
1849	27	manic
1854+	0	suicide attempt
Other years:	average 3–5	

Table 3.12: Work composed by Schumann in different years of his life

Tennyson, who suffered from Bipolar Disorder. His father and grandfather on his father's side showed symptoms, and seven of Tennyson's eleven siblings had some form of mood disorder.

When trying to establish if some behaviour is inherited, there are two main methods of research used:

- twin studies
- adoption studies.

Twin studies focus on the similarity in behaviour (known as the concordance rate) between the two twins. MZ (identical) twins share the same genes, which means that any similarity in behaviour could be down to genes. DZ (non-identical) twins share only 50% of the same genes. In the main, we would expect the concordance rates of MZ twins to be higher than DZ for the behaviour to be seen as genetically based. The studies on MZ twins tend to find concordance rates between 65% and 80%, with between 15% and 25% for DZ twins. The difference in rates between studies depends on the definition of the Bipolar Disorder and the size of the sample.

With adoption studies, researchers are interested in children of parent(s) with Bipolar Disorder who are adopted by non-sufferers. This removes the influence of the environment, which means that if the children still develop the illness, it will be genetic. The problem is that such situations are limited, particularly because these studies are based on volunteers often. For example, Cadoret (1978) found only 8 adopted children from biological parent(s) with Bipolar Disorder. Of these children, 3 developed a mood disorder as an adult. This figure is about 40%. This compares with only 8 of 126 who developed mood disorders from non-Bipolar Disorders biological parents (around 5%). Both twin studies and adoption studies have weaknesses (see Table 3.13).

Current research is attempting to find the gene that may be involved. For example, Escamilla *et al* (1999) report a study with a Costa Rican family tree, where Bipolar Disorder is very high. They feel that chromosome 18 is involved. Work with the Amish community in the USA has highlighted chromosome 11 (Egeland *et al*, 1987). However, there are

Problems with twin studies

1 In many cases diagnoses are made retrospectively and based on records rather than with the actual individual.

2 Some of the sample may in fact be dead and guesses are made about the illness.

3 Small sample sizes of the studies (e.g. around 20 pairs of twins).

4 Different definitions of the illnesses.

5 Volunteers.

Problems with adoption studies

1 The age of adoption – i.e. how much time is spent with the biological parents (and thus the influence of the environment).

2 Retrospective diagnoses.

3 Small sample size.

4 Different definitions of illnesses.

5 Volunteers.

Table 3.13: Problems with twin studies and adoption studies

The poet Tennyson: genetically disposed to Bipolar Disorder

family tree studies that do not support either of these findings.

Commentary

In the same way as depression is linked to SAD, there is evidence of a rare condition called 'seasonal mania', which is where individuals show manic symptoms only during the summer months.

Neurochemistry

One area of research has been the biochemistry of the brain. Schildkraut (1970), for example, proposed the Norepinephrine Theory, which suggests that a lack of norepinephrine (noradrenaline) causes depression and an excess equals mania.

Other neurochemical causes have been suggested since then. There is limited support for these ideas because drugs working on these neurochemicals stop the symptoms. However, it is not clear whether the symptoms are caused by the neurochemicals or vice versa.

Commentary

Browne *et al* (2000) traced 76 individuals born in Dublin who were diagnosed with mania between 1972–86, and compared them to a control group. Birth difficulties were found to not be a risk factor for mania.

Schizophrenia

This is the best known mental illness, yet least understood by people generally. When people talk of 'madness', they are usually thinking of schizophrenia, or 'schizo' as used in everyday language (often as an insult).

There are many misconceptions about schizophrenia. The first of these is the everyday belief that schizophrenics are dangerous to others, and likely to commit crime. In a Camberwell study, Wessely (1997) found the rate of crime among schizophrenics to be no different to the general population (substance misuse being the group with the highest rate). Because of the few rare attacks on strangers that have been publicized, a general impression of danger has been created. Individuals are more likely to be attacked by someone they know or, if the attacker is a stranger, the stranger is unlikely to be suffering from schizophrenia. Eight times as many murders (under section 2 of the Homicide Act) are committed by non-sufferers of mental illness in the UK. The MacArthur Violence Risk Assessment Study of 1000 patients and 500 controls in Pitts-burgh and Kansas found schizophrenia to have the lowest rate of violence among any psychotic disorder. There is a much greater risk of schizophrenics injuring themselves than anyone else.

The second misconception is that schizophrenia is a single disorder, but, in fact, it is more like a syndrome – that is, a combination of different symptoms (and disorders). DSM IV talks about schizophrenic disorders, as well as schizotypal behaviour (which is a milder variation).

Incidence of schizophrenia

It is estimated that there are 1 million sufferers of schizophrenic disorders in the UK and around 2 million sufferers in the USA. This works out at a risk level of 1 in 100 of the adult population.

However, the prevalence rates do vary between urban and rural areas, and across ethnic groups. In the largest study in the UK in recent years, a comparison was made between Nithsdale (a rural area in south-west Scotland), and Nunhead and Norwood (south London) – with Nunhead being classed as an inner-city area (see Table 3.14).

Rates have also been found to vary between countries. For example, Jablensky *et al* (1992) found a low incidence rate of 0.5% of the population (aged 15–54 years) in Honolulu (Hawaii) to 1.7% in rural India. The rate for Moscow was 1.1% compared to 0.8% for Nottingham.

Schizophrenia usually appears in the teen years, but can come in childhood or adulthood. Men have the highest risk before age 25, while for women, it is after 25 (Lovanger, 1984).

Schizophrenic disorders can be episodic (that is, periods of the disorder and periods without), or they can be one single recoverable or non-recoverable attack. Between one-third and a quarter of suf-

	Nithsdale		Nunhead	Norwood
White	2.50		3.00	2.00
Non-white	–		6.00	5.00
Male	4.75	white	4.00	2.50
		non-white	11.50	9.25
Female	2.00	white	2.00	1.50
		non-white	7.00	6.00

McCreadie, 1997.

Table 3.14: Approximate rates of schizophrenia per 10,000 people in three different areas of the UK (based on DSM IIIR and ICD 10 criteria)

ferers make a recovery from an acute attack. In practice, one-third of sufferers recover after one episode and never experience another attack, one-third have relapses and episodes throughout their lives, and one-third never recover from the initial attack of the illness. Relapse is less likely in patients with insight about their illness, who have minimal stress and who are compliant with drugs given.

Characteristics of schizophrenia

Kraeplin (1919) used the term 'dementia praecox' (meaning the premature appearance of derangement common in old age), while Bleuler coined the term 'schizophrenia' to mean the splitting of the mind – that is, a split between thought and emotions. It is not the same as multiple personality.

Stafford-Clark (1984) emphasizes the 'progressive disintegration of emotional stability, judgement, contact with, and appreciation of reality', while the National Schizophrenia Fellowship points out the 'splitting or internal disturbances and distortions within the sufferer's thought processes, feelings and perceptions'. Overall the whole personality is affected, though the symptoms are fluid and changing. This can make diagnosis difficult.

Diagnosis in the UK tends to be based on 'first rank symptoms' (Schneider, 1959) – the presence of at least one of the following three symptoms (and no brain damage evident).

1 Passivity of experience and thought disturbances: sufferers believes their thoughts are being interfered with in some way – for example, 'thought insertion' from outside or that their thoughts are being broadcast like a radio station. The sufferers often talk about their experiences as if they are someone else.

2 Auditory hallucinations: hearing voices when no one else is physically present. These voices may be talking about the sufferer, or they could be commanding or threatening. But it is argued that auditory hallucinations are not automatically a sign of schizophrenia. Often it is the interpretation of the voices that is important – for example, telepathy, alien communications, or a 'little voice inside' that the individual fails to notice is self-generated.

3 Primary delusions: sufferers hold certain beliefs despite obvious contrary evidence – for example, 'delusions of grandeur'. Here, the individual firmly believes that he (or she) is some great his-

torical figure or that his life matters today. Another example is 'delusions of reference', which is the belief that the news on television is about the individual. Other delusions can revolve around having committed the 'unpardonable sin', or in fact to be dead and observing the world as a ghost.

Slater and Roth (1959) see hallucinations as the least important symptom because they are also present in other disorders. Slater and Roth prefer to include other symptoms in their diagnosis, such as:

- thought process disorder – for example, inability to concentrate
- disturbance of affect – for example, wrong emotions shown; anger or self-criticism for no apparent reason
- psychomotor disorders – for example, strange postures or lack of movement
- lack of violation or will – for example, apathetic to the point of not getting out of bed.

There are many additional symptoms that accompany the main 'core' symptoms. In fact, criticisms have been made of the large number of possible symptoms. For convenience, two main types of schizophrenia are diagnosed by clinicians:

- type I, with 'positive symptoms' – including hallucinations and delusions (similar to mania)
- type II, with 'negative symptoms' – including inactivity or flatness of emotions (similar to depression).

So, in fact, sufferers can show entirely different symptoms and still be diagnosed as having a schizophrenic disorder.

The classification systems tend to note five main kinds of schizophrenia, as follows:

1 Simple schizophrenia: this develops in late adolescence with a gradual onset. It involves a deterioration of social behaviour, increased apathy, and difficulty in making friends. Sufferers start missing appointments and eventually do not leave their beds. Consequently they may lose jobs or their accommodation, which could lead to homelessness.

2 Hebephrenic (disorganized) schizophrenia: this kind appears in people aged in their early 20s. It has a number of the symptoms common with simple schizophrenia, but, in particular, behaviour is often silly or childish. There may be disorganized speech and behaviour.

3 Catatonic schizophrenia: the characteristics of this kind are either excited violent motor behaviour or mute stupors. It often involves doing the opposite to what is asked or repeating everything that is said.

4 Paranoid schizophrenia: in some ways, this is the least severe of the kinds of schizophrenia, though it is the best known. Delusions of grandeur and/or persecution are the key characteristics.

5 Residential/undifferentiated schizophrenia: the classification systems also have a 'catch all' category for sufferers who do not fit the other kinds. In practice, it is often difficult to distinguish the kind of schizophrenia.

DSM IIIR emphasizes phases in the diagnosis process. First is the prodromal phase, where there is a clear deterioration in the individual's behaviour. Next is the residual phase, with the persistence of at least two symptoms or remission of the symptoms. Finally, there's the active phase, where the symptoms are prominent.

Commentary

Peter Chadwick, who has suffered from schizophrenic disorders himself, argues in his book *Schizophrenia: The Positive Perspective* about the concept of 'schizophrenic credit'. This is a state that 'gives one the sense of accessing 'the elsewhere'' … a glimpse into the deep structure of reality …'.

Chadwick believes that sufferers are more aware of certain things like the patterns of events in life (synchronicity), or are able to detect deception via facial cues better. There is also a 'creativity bonus'; indeed, many famous writers and artists have suffered from schizophrenic or schizotypal disorders – for example Tennessee Williams and Ezra Pound.

Explanations of schizophrenia

For a long time, the causes of schizophrenia were addressed as the nature or nurture debate. Either it was due to genetics or the environment. This is too simple, and in practice nobody stands on one side only. Realistically it is a combination of both.

Vulnerability model
This model argues that there is a predisposition to schizophrenia that is inherited, but it needs the appropriate environmental conditions (that is, stressful) to trigger the manifestation of the disorder.

First, looking for the genetic predisposition,

research has used twin studies, adoption studies and gene research. There have been a number of twin studies, some more reliable than others, and they find different concordance rates (that is, levels of similarity between the twins). There is no definite study, but they all show that genetics plays a part in the cause of schizophrenia. For example, the concordance rates for MZ (identical) twins reared apart varies from 6% to 86%, while for DZ (non-identical) twins reared together, the rates vary from 2% to 34%. But many of these studies have small samples.

Adoption studies with children from biological parent(s) with schizophrenia adopted by non-schizophrenic individuals have also found some influence of genetics. A number of studies have been made in Scandinavia, where detailed records are kept. For example, the Finnish Adoption Study, begun in 1969, followed 112 adoptees with a biological mother suffering from schizophrenia, and 135 control adoptees, all separated before four years old. Tienari et al (1987) found schizophrenia diagnosed in 7% of the experimental group and 1.5% of the control group. Breggin (1991) points out that where the adoptees had developed schizophrenia, it was found that the adopted parent(s) were suffering from a mental disorder. So it could be due to the effect of the environment. Adoption studies also have methodological weaknesses (see Table 3.13, page 52).

Overall the risk of developing schizophrenia is around 40% for a child where both parents are sufferers. This compares to a risk of 1% in the general population. However, a majority of such children do not develop the disorder, so the environment must play a role. The role of the environment as the stressor that triggers the predisposition to schizophrenia has focused on poverty and family interactions.

Concentrating on poverty first, the argument runs that such a situation is very stressful and this triggers the appearance of schizophrenia. Early research simply compared the percentage of those in psychiatric hospitals by social class. For example, Hollingshead and Redlich (1958) found in their Connecticut (USA) study that only 1% of the top social class were in hospital compared to 37% of the lowest social class. The problem with this type of study is that it is not clear on the causes and effects – for example, is poverty the cause of schizophrenia, or does schizophrenia cause the individual to drift into poverty?

In the 1960s, the focus was on the family as the cause of many problems. In particular, the communication patterns and expression of emotions in certain families was seen as unhealthy. Fontana (1966) noted more aggression between parents of a schizophrenic child than a control group, and less communication with that offspring. Fromm-Reichman (1948) coined the phrase 'schizophrenogic families', where there is high emotional tension, secrets and conspiracies within the family. Bateson *et al* (1956) highlighted a communication style called 'double bind', where the child receives conflicting messages from the parents – for example, a parent shouting 'I love you' while beating the child.

However, the communication patterns in the family may have changed with the appearance of schizophrenia rather than being the cause of it. Certainly, recent research has shown that 'high negative emotional expression' (EE) and 'communication deviance' (CD) are crucial in the relapse of sufferers. Vaughn and Leff (1976) report studies showing a relapse rate as high as 70% in this situation.

Anti-psychiatry model

A completely different explanation comes from the work of RD Laing in the 1960s. He argued that schizophrenia was not a disease but a problem with living. In fact, schizophrenics are more sane than normal people because the normal state of mind in industrial society is 'alienation' (that is, to suppress feelings and adopt a 'false self').

Schizophrenia is 'hypersanity' – that is, a voyage into another reality to find an authentic identity. The individual becomes labelled as schizophrenic, and this role is reinforced by others. In time, the individual comes to accept the label, and thus becomes schizophrenic.

Laing, who was a trained psychiatrist, tried to get inside the heads of sufferers and assumed that what they said was intelligent to them. This was a radical approach in the 1960s.

Laing wrote three main books on the subject, and through these it is possible to trace the development of his ideas. In the *Divided Self* (1959) Laing talks about 'ontological insecurity', which occurs when the individual experiences a split between the world and the self. One type of 'ontological insecurity' is engulfment – a dread of being swallowed up by others if involvement is too close.

In the *Self and Others* (1961), Laing focused on the conspiratorial model of mental illness. Here, he emphasized the use of labels by doctors for those who were non-conformist.

Laing's third book on the subject, *The Politics of Experience* (1967), outlines the voyage into themselves that schizophrenics should be allowed to take in order to heal themselves. But society does not normally let them take this voyage.

This is a very different view of schizophrenia to the medical model, but its support is limited today. The dominance of drug treatments has meant that the medical model is the prevailing view, particularly as the drugs seem to produce an improvement in symptoms for many sufferers.

Table 3.15 summarizes briefly the main other explanations for schizophrenia.

Eating disorders

Eating disorders are a growing category of behav-

RD Laing: his radical approach to schizophrenia implied that schizophrenics were more sane than 'normal' people

Neuroanatomy	With the improvement in medical technology (for example, CAT scans), studies are finding brain structure differences in schizophrenics; areas involved include the anterior cingulate gyrus and the prefrontal cortex
Neurochemical	In the 1970s the dopamine hypothesis, which argued that an excess of dopamine was the cause of schizophrenia was popular; focus on any one neurochemical is now seen as too simplistic
Cognitive	Misattribution of own thoughts as from outside – e.g. auditory hallucinations are normal voices in the head not monitored as so

Table 3.15: Other main explanations for schizophrenia

1 Determined food avoidance.

2 Weight loss or failure to gain appropriate weight (if aged 10–14 years).

3 2+ of the following:

　a preoccupation with body weight

　b preoccupation with energy intake

　c distorted body image

　d self-induced vomiting

　e extensive exercising

　f purging (including laxative abuse).

Table 3.16: Great Ormond Street Hospital diagnostic checklist

iours related to problems with food. These disorders may relate to eating too much or eating too little at the extremes. Anorexia nervosa and bulimia nervosa are the best known forms of eating disorders. Pye (1996) highlights the common characteristics of all eating disorders as:

- the abuse of food in some way
- the problem with food being an expression of another problem
- leading to changes in personality or personal habits
- leading to lapses in friendship and resulting social isolation.

Other measures include the Great Ormond Street Hospital Checklist (see Table 3.16) and the SCOFF questionnaire (see Table 3.17).

Launer (2000) points out that sufferers 'each make the fundamental error of believing that weight, or lack of it, is connected to emotional well-

1 Do you make yourself SICK because you feel uncomfortably full?

2 Do you worry you have lost CONTROL over how much you eat?

3 Have you recently lost more than ONE stone in a three-month period?

4 Do you believe yourself to be FAT when others say you are too thin?

5 Would you say that FOOD dominates your life?

Scoring: 1 point for each statement agreed with; total of 2 or more = signs of eating disorder.

Morgan *et al*, 1999.

Table 3.17: SCOFF questionnaire

Food Avoidance Emotional Disorder (FAED)	partial anorexia
Food refusal	no preoccupation with body weight
Pervasive refusal	refusal to eat, drink, walk, talk and care for self
Selective eating	eating only particular foods
Appetite loss secondary to depression	
Subclinical Eating Disorder (SED)	preoccupation with weight but not to extreme of anorexia
Abnormal Weight Syndrome	feeling fat though not – i.e. no bingeing but vomiting etc
Binge Eating Disorder	bulimia without guilt and panic – i.e. just binge eating
Normal Weight Bulimia (NWB)	near normal weight female with bulimia symptoms

Table 3.18: Less well known eating disorders

being' (p. 131). In other words, their weight and food become the key to their whole state of mind. There are many different types of eating disorders (see Table 3.18), which are variations on anorexia and bulimia (see Table 3.19).

The prevalence of these eating disorders is difficult to establish because many sufferers do not seek help, and the form of the disorder may be mild. Bulimia, in particular, is often a secretive disorder, where sufferers can hide their behaviour even from close family members.

	Bulimia	Anorexia
Age of onset	16–45 (mainly 20–25)	teen years
Background of sufferer	mixed	predominantly middle class
Personality	extrovert, socially competent, and sexually experienced	introvert, sexually inexperienced
Appearance	normal range	thin
Depression	severe/self-disgust	not so bad
Similarities	– extreme concert about shape and weight	
	– behaviour designed to control body weight	

Table 3.19: Comparison of bulimia and anorexia nervosa

Cooper and Fairburn (1983) gave out questionnaires to women of all ages at a family planning clinic. Some 20.6% reported eating problems of some kind and 26.4% admitted to having binge eaten at some stage. Some 85% of the women were within the normal weight range, yet 60% reported feeling fat.

Among teenagers, Whitaker *et al* (1990) found anorexia to be self-reported at 0.2% and bulimia 2.5% of the 5500 sample. But these studies are self-reported.

Though the number of women with actual eating disorders may be small, many women want to lose weight or feel fat when objectively not so. In a massive survey of 30,000 9–16 year old girls, Charter (1998) found that 60% wanted to lose weight, but only 15% of the sample were objectively overweight. Similarly, in a survey of 106 Australian women (aged 19–29) 47% wanted to be a 'little lighter' and 32% 'a lot lighter'. Among 44 bulimia patients, the figures were 18% and 64% respectively (Abraham and Llewellyn-Jones, 1992).

Commentary

Most of the research and public awareness has been on teenage women, but eating disorders exist among other groups. Approximately 20% (depending on the study) of gay men also suffer (see RLA 15). Gay men show a high level of body dissatisfaction, which is common among female sufferers. In a comparison of 41 young gay and 41 heterosexual men in Britain, Williamson and Hartley (1998) found a significant difference on EAT-26 and the Body Satisfaction Scale (BSS). EAT-26 is a questionnaire designed to measure eating and dieting behaviour, and BSS measures satisfaction with the physical body.

Real Life Application 15:

A body to die for

Juan Rivera was a chubby 16 year old when he 'came out'. But very quickly afterwards he started to lose weight by drinking coffee, smoking and not eating (except cereals occasionally). He died aged 26 of dehydration and gastroenteritis. But he was male, gay and Latino, nothing like the typical victim of anorexia.

Over 10% of all anorexia sufferers are men, and this proportion is on the increase. The figure for bulimia may be nearer 40%.

Victoria Stagg Elliott reports a London case of a 26 year old gay man who had spent ten years of his life with bulimia. He would eat a large pizza, a tub of ice cream, garlic bread, another large pizza, biscuits and sandwiches in one sitting. Then he would stick his fingers down his throat or spin around and around in order to be sick. He was so ashamed because for him, men didn't suffer from bulimia. The sufferer looking back partly blames the 'body fascism' of the London gay scene. Also his 'coming out' made his mother seriously ill, and he felt he must punish himself for that.

Gay Times, August 1997.

Summary

- Traditionally it was felt that only women suffered from eating disorders, but more and more sufferers are men, and in particular gay men.

Questions

1 What does the sufferer of bulimia from London mean by 'body fascism'?

2 What are the key symptoms of bulimia shown by the London sufferer?

3 What is the traditional image of an anorexia sufferer?

Anorexia nervosa

Among mental disorders, this has the highest death rate – between 10% and 20% of sufferers. Many of these deaths are due to complications through lack of food, but some are suicides. Some 20% of sufferers have a single episode with full recovery, and 60% episodes and relapses. Steinhausen (1997) reviewed 31 studies on the outcome of 941 young anorexia sufferers in the long term. Some 51.5% made a 'good' recovery, and 28.8% 'fair' (improvement). Overall only 52% returned to 'normal eating behaviour', and 67.6% to 'normal weight'.

DSM IV bases diagnosis on four criteria, as outlined below:

- Refusal to maintain minimally normal body weight.
- Intense fear of gaining weight despite being underweight.
- Disturbance in the way body shape/weight is experienced – for example, overemphasis for self-evaluation.

- The absence of three consecutive menstruations.

Despite the sufferers' refusal to eat, they are obsessed with food. This could include collecting recipes and preparing lavish meals for others.

The children's television presenter Michaela Strachen suffered from anorexia nervosa when she was eighteen years old. It began as a 'sensible diet' when she went to music college. However, it developed into an eating disorder with vomiting, laxative use and excessive exercise. Michaela might only have eaten a dry roll, an apple and a grapefruit during the day. She reports looking in the mirror and always seeing weight that had to be lost. She compared herself to fatter women who she thought were thinner. She rarely ate from a plate, but would eat from boxes and rubbish bins, and others' leftovers because these were not proper meals. She could not eat in front of other people. The causes are multiple – including the break-up of her parents' marriage, not wanting to take responsibility as an adult, and control being important in her life (*Enemy Within*, 1995).

Precipitating factors in anorexia nervosa

Slade (1982) has identified factors that precede an episode of anorexia. These are outlined below:

1 Low self-esteem: the sufferer tends to have low self-esteem caused by many possible many reasons – family problems, changes in adolescence, relationships with the opposite sex, too high expectations by the family and thus the individual themselves.
2 Perfectionist tendencies.
3 The need for complete control, and the body can be rigidly controlled.
4 A specific psycho-stimuli – that is, a trigger comment about body shape.

The individual gains positive reinforcement from succeeding in controlling the body in dieting, and this increases the self-esteem. But this is not enough because of the unobtainable goals of the perfectionist. The family can reinforce the behaviour by the attention they give the sufferer, or because family problems are pushed under the carpet.

Prolonged starvation has major consequences for the body including amenorrhoea (absence of menstruation), brittle bones that break easily, muscles that become weak, difficulty in concentrating and sleeping, and depression. In fact the whole body is affected (see Table 3.20). The immediate treatment in severe sufferers is weight increase (see RLA 16).

Mineral	How deficiency develops	Effect
Calcium	less dairy products or excessive exercise	osteoporosis (brittle bones)
Iron	less red meat	anaemia
Potassium/ phosphate	tissue loss	cardiac failure

Table 3.20: Mineral deficiencies in anorexia

Real Life Application 16:
Telling the full story

Rhodes Farm in North London is a specialist clinic for teenagers with anorexia. It was started in 1991 by Dr. Dee Dawson.

Though the atmosphere is relaxed like a big house, the regime is strict. The patients must put on a kilogram a week as determined by a specific diet.

Mealtimes are difficult as the patients have to eat. For most of them this is a horrific experience. It is not force-feeding, but strong psychological pressure and encouragement is used. After the meal, patients have to stay downstairs to stop them vomiting and exercising. The reward for successful patients is 'freedom' – that is, days out or weekends away.

At the same time, there is therapy to deal with the underlying problems.

Adapted from 'Telling the full story' by Vicki Ward, *The Guardian*, 22 June 1999.

Summary

- Rhodes Farm Clinic uses a two-prong attack to help anorexics – making sure that they eat for their physical needs, and therapy for the underlying emotional problems.

Questions

1 On what principles is the clinic mainly based?

2 Why is it necessary to have therapy as well as making the patients eat?

3 Name another technique that has been used to help anorexics when their weight is low.

Bulimia nervosa

Bulimia manifests itself in a number of forms and may appear as well as anorexia (technically known as co-morbidity). The key characteristics are episodes of binge eating followed by compensatory behaviour – for example, self-induced vomiting.

The binge will involve much more than a large meal, even as much as 20,000 calories in one session. In one example, a sufferer ate two packets of biscuits, a loaf of bread, a gallon of ice cream, a fried chicken and cakes, and drank a gallon of milk (Davison and Neale, 1990). Bulimia is not about being hungry because sufferers eat far more food than would be required to satisfy normal hunger. The sufferers are usually within the normal weight range.

DSM IV emphasizes the binge–purge cycle, which must occur more than twice a week over a three-month period. The purging type of bulimia includes self-induced vomiting or laxatives, while non-purging is based on fasting and excessive exercise to remove the binge.

Gomez (1995) tries to pin down the state of mind preceding the binge – for example:

- a vague uneasiness when alone
- loneliness and boredom
- resentment
- anxiety and disappointment
- feelings of lack of appreciation.

Other researchers highlight the cyclical nature of the disorder (see Figure 3.8).

The excessive use of laxatives and self-induced vomiting on a regular basis have consequences for the body. These include:

- stomach acid dissolving enamel on teeth
- puffy face (due to swollen salivary glands)
- damage to bowel muscles, which may lead to long-term constipation
- kidney damage
- lack of protein.

Researchers have been able to identify risk factors for sufferers of this disorder, as outlined below.

- Features of the family: including poor communication, unease and vague dissatisfaction, and problems hidden.
- Mother: limited relationship with sufferer, a succession of male partners, own weight problems, rewarded her unhappiness with food.
- Father: possibly alcoholic, and distant.

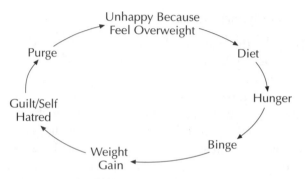

Figure 3.8: Cycle of behaviour in bulimia

- Sufferer: childhood sexual abuse, tendency towards depression and/or substance abuse.
- Society: pressure to be slim, conflicting messages about food, and gender role conflicts.
- Certain professions: those where appearance important – for example, modelling.

Shisslak *et al* (1986) believe there are four misconceptions in the thinking of sufferers, as below:

1 Their appearance is the sole criterion of evaluation by others.
2 They must devote themselves to fulfilling the desire of others.
3 Emotional expression of personal needs is unacceptable.
4 They will be unloved unless perfect.

Explanations for eating disorders

Explanations of eating disorders include physiological differences of the sufferers compared to non-sufferers, and the socio-culturist and feminist issues. The text that follows examines these two explanations in more details.

Physiological differences

Current research is seeking a biological basis of eating disorders – that is, a physiological difference in sufferers compared to non-sufferers. A number of different symptoms within the body have been studied.

The main focus is the hypothalamus, which is the part of the brain linked to eating, drinking and sexual behaviour (among other things). Work with rats found that damage to this area produces a change in eating behaviours. If the ventro-medial hypothalamus is damaged, the rat will not stop eating, while with the lateral hypothalamus the rats cease to eat despite the presence of food. Literally they will starve to death. It may be that anorexics have some kind of damage to the lateral hypothalamus. However, post-mortems on anorexics have found no such damage.

An alternative physiological cause of anorexia could be serotonin disturbances. Serotonin is a neurotransmitter linked to many behaviours and mood. A high level of serotonin tends to reduce the motivation to eat (that is, it behaves as an appetite suppressant). The high level of serotonin may be caused by high anxiety, and the reduction in food means a reduction in the chemical trytophan (found in food), which reduces the anxiety (*Horizon*, 1999).

In a different way, Abraham and Llewellyn-Jones (1992) explain bingeing through low levels of trytophan. This can be increased by large carbohydrate intakes, as in bingeing, which increases the serotonin levels and mood. In their study, the researchers increased the levels of trytophan in a number of bulimics, who reduced their bingeing.

Alternatively, Kennedy (1997) reports research that sixteen out of eighteen anorexic teenagers had less blood flow to the anterior or temporal lobe, which are the parts of the brain that govern visual perception, appetite and sense of fullness.

Other suggestions have included nutritional influences. For example, Dalvitt-McPhillips (1984) found that 20 bulimic women placed on nutrient-dense diets with food additives removed for six weeks ceased to binge and maintained this state for up to two years.

There is no clear-cut physiological explanation for eating disorders. Furthermore, many of the physiological changes could be a product of the change in eating behaviour of the disorders rather than the causes.

Socio-cultural/feminist explanation

This explanation for eating disorders looks at the social context and, in particular, the images of women presented in the media. Eating disorders are most prevalent in industrial societies where there is an abundance of food but an ideal of slimness. Orbach (1987) argues that this is an oppressive pressure for thinness directed at women.

This message is communicated in the images in society, like in magazines. Malkin *et al* (1999) performed a content analysis on the covers of 21 women's and men's magazines for messages about bodily appearance. One-third of the women's magazines mentioned diets compared to none of the men's. It is noticeable that models became smaller in the second half of the twentieth century. Spitzer *et al* (1999) compared the average weights of winners of the 'Miss America' competition. The average weight in the 1950s was 56 kilograms compared to 50 kilograms in the 1980s.

Feminists focus on how these images affect the experience of women and the traditional emphasis on caring for the family. This means that the woman's own desires are secondary, and her self-identity becomes based around the association with a man – that is, a wife is defined by her husband.

Models weigh less today than 50 years ago

Genetic	Some evidence for genetics – e.g. up to ten times more likely to develop eating disorders if first-degree relative suffered; the genetic link may be to personality or mood, which cause the eating disorder
Personality	Bruch (1974) argues that eating disorders are caused by underlying personality disorder, which includes disturbed body image (i.e. delusional about weight), inability to assess accurately bodily sensations of hunger and fullness, and 'paralysing sense of ineffectiveness'; the personality disorder is due to early difficulties in the parent–child relationship
Psychodynamic	Fear and desperation for intimacy not gained in childhood manifests itself as fears of poisoning, and starvation
Evolutionary	In the evolutionary past when food was short, it was an advantage to control appetite and ignore hanger pangs, then binge when food was available; this evolutionary mechanism is maladaptive in modern society with the regular availability of food
Family	Moorey (1991) talks of 'anorexic families' where there is a lack of conflict resolution, marital disillusionment, self-sacrifice and enmeshment (over-involvement between family members with no privacy); starvation is used by the child as a weapon against parental conflict
'Regression model'	Anorexia as a desire to avoid sexual maturity and a rejection of womanhood
Cognitive	Faulty thinking patterns – e.g. 'I must be thin to be loved'; perceptual distortions – e.g. overestimating own weight and body shape

Table 3.21: Other main explanations of eating disorders

However, this is changing and producing conflicting messages for women – for example, juggling their own desires and caring for family at same time, while remaining thin and beautiful. Thus, starvation can be seen as an attempt at control in a world lacking control.

Petkova (1997) suggests the problem lies in the actual social construction of femininity; men exert pressure on women to be thin. Wolf (1991) calls this the 'Professional Beauty Qualification'. But the media representations of female beauty are unrealistic and unobtainable. This situation creates a form of 'double bind' again with conflicting messages.

The whole emphasis of this explanation is outside the sufferer. Other support comes from the fact that, though only a relatively small number of women have diagnosed eating disorders, the vast majority are concerned about weight and dieting. One Californian study estimated that 80% of nine year old girls were, or had been, on a diet.

In the case of gay men who suffer from eating disorders, there is a similar pattern. In the gay media, men are presented as the ideal of slim, boyish and physically attractive ('Ganymede archetype', Wright, 1997). This is unrealistic and also unobtainable. Williamson (1999) argues that eating disorders among gay men are 'internalized homo-negativity' – that is, the internalization of society's homophobia.

However, the socio-cultural explanation is probably not the only cause of eating disorders by itself. Table 3.21 summarizes briefly the other main explanations for eating disorders.

Conclusions on eating disorders

Researchers and practitioners working with eating disorder sufferers tend to build a model with multiple causes. Eating disorders are complex behaviours and single explanations are probably too simplistic. One way to view eating disorders is at the three different levels that follow:

1 Personal vulnerability: there are certain factors that make some individuals more vulnerable to developing eating disorders than others. The factors include a tendency to perfectionism, low self-esteem, traumatic childhood experience (for example, sexual abuse), and/or childhood obesity.

2 Precipitating factors: there are triggers that can set off the developing of eating disorders. These include the experience of puberty and the physical changes, stressful life events and/or successful dieting with social reinforcement for weight loss (for example, images of slim models).

3 Perpetuating factors: factors that work to continue the behaviour, such as lack of satisfaction with weight loss, body image distortion leading to fear of returning to normal weight, depression and anxiety from starvation and/or fear of living without the eating disorder.

Essay questions

1 Compare and contrast the explanations of phobias.

2 Discuss the research on eating disorders.

3 Discuss the importance of genetic and environmental influences on schizophrenia.

④ Treatments and therapies

This chapter looks at how the different approaches to abnormal behaviour attempt to help individuals to 'get better'. Details of the main treatments and therapies are outlined with their strengths and weaknesses. The treatments are based on the medical model, and the therapies based on the psychodynamic, behavioural, cognitive and humanistic models. Real Life Applications that are considered are:

- RLA 17: Is it time for my Prozac, mum?
- RLA 18: Shock, horror or help?

Traditionally, a distinction is made between physical treatments (based on the medical model) and therapies (which focus on the psychological). Another distinction can be made between directive techniques, like behaviour therapy (which tell the client what to do) and non-directive, like psychoanalysis. There is also the difference between action and insight, and techniques can be either individual or group based. Table 4.1 summarizes these differences.

The term 'psychotherapy' is often used in books, but it is ambiguous. Originally it meant psychodynamic-based therapy, but it is now often used to mean any therapy. Gelder et al (1995) prefer to divide the types of therapies into four groups, as follows:

- Relief of distress and maintenance function – for example, listening.
- Readjustment – for example, humanistic.
- Restoration of function – for example, behaviour techniques, CBT.
- Reconstruction – for example, psychodynamic.

Treatments

These are techniques based on the medical model.

Several terms are used, including somatic, organic or physical treatments. Their aim is to produce a physical change in the physiology of the sufferer. The underlying basis of the medical model is discussed in Chapter 2 (see pages 15–26). This section focuses on the three main treatments:

- psychotropic drugs
- electro-convulsive therapy (ECT)
- psychosurgery.

Psychotropic drugs

The use of drugs to treat mental illness appeared in the 1950s and 60s with the development of research on the neuron, synapse and neurotransmitters in the brain. Drugs work by altering the brain's chemistry, which is seen as the cause of mental illness. For example, depression could be due to a shortage of serotonin, so anti-depressants work by increasing the amount of serotonin. Drugs can be administered orally or by depot preparation (that is, injection). The latter technique is for patients who are not willing to comply with their drugs or who may forget to take them. Some drugs, like chlorpromazine, have suppository versions.

	Treatment/ therapy	Directive/ non-directive	Action/ insight	Individual/ group
Medical	Tr	N/A	N/A	Ind
Psychodynamic	Th	Non	In	Both, mainly ind
Behaviour	Th	Dir	Act	Mainly ind
Cognitive	Th	Dir	Act	Both
Humanistic	Th	Non	In	Both

Table 4.1: Summary of differences between main treatments and therapies

In Britain there is a legal limit for alcohol intake when driving, but not for psychotropic drugs. Tests have been made on stopping distance by Ian Hindmarsh at the University of Surrey.

Extra stopping distance at 70 mph:

Legal limit of alcohol	8 feet
Tricyclic anti-depressants (e.g. dothiepin)	10 feet

It has been estimated that drivers taking tricyclic anti-depressants (TCA) are six times more likely to have an accident than drivers not taking them. The problem is not the same for selective serotonin reuptake inhibitors (SSRI).

World in Action, 1994.

Figure 4.1: A fatal prescription

Though there are many different psychotropic drugs, the three main groups are:

- anti-depressants
- neuroleptics
- anti-anxiety drugs.

Anti-depressants
As the name implies, this group of drugs, of which there are many different types, are used with depression. 'First-generation' anti-depressants appeared in the 1960s in two main forms:

- tricyclics (TCA)
- mono-oxidize inhibitors (MAOI).

Unfortunately, the latter interact with certain foods, so a strict diet is required when taking these drugs.

The biggest problem with 'first-generation' anti-depressants has been the side effects, which can be severe. These can include dizziness, blurred vision, dry mouth, constipation, weight gain, cardiac problems and a risk when driving (see Figure 4.1). They are also toxic (that is, overdose is possible), but not addictive.

The 'second generation' of anti-depressants appeared in the 1980s, and includes a group known as selective serotonin reuptake inhibitors (SSRI). Best known of these is the brand name Prozac (manufactured by Eli Lilley). SSRIs have less side effects than the 'first generation', and overdosing is now more difficult. The original claims of no side effects by the manufacturers has been proved wrong.

Research on anti-depressants has focused on the efficacy (that is, effectiveness) of the drug, and whether one type of anti-depressant is better than another. The findings tend to agree that anti-depressants are better than placebo, but no particular anti-depressant is better than another (Spigset and Martensson, 1999). The only differences are side effects and the cost. For example, SSRIs can be up to eight times more expensive than TCAs. New anti-depressants – for example, serotonin and nora-drenaline reuptake inhibitors (SNRI) – are being produced all the time. But all of them take a period of about two to four weeks before the onset of an effect (see Table 4.2).

Neuroleptics (major tranquillizers/anti-pyschotic drugs
This group of drugs is mainly used for psychotic illness, like schizophrenia, and aims generally to reduce the amount of certain neurochemicals. The major problem has always been the high level of side effects.

The most disturbing side effects are known technically as anticholonergic effects and extrapyramidal side effects (EPSE). The former symptoms include dry mouth, blurred vision and constipation, while the latter includes tardive dyskinesia (uncontrollable muscle twitching and spasms), including tongue protusions (see Table 4.3, page 66).

Name	Overdose rating	Onset of effects	Level of side effects	Cost
TCA e.g. imipramine	high	2–6 weeks	high	cheap
MAOI e.g. phenelzine	high	1–4 weeks	high	cheapest
SSRI e.g. fluoxetine	medium	2–4 weeks	medium	expensive
SNRI e.g. venlafaxine	medium	2–4 weeks	medium	high

Data based on 'BMA: New Guide to Medicine and Drugs'.

Table 4.2: Comparison of different types of anti-depressants

Name	Antichol	EPSE	Overdose	Onset
Phenothiazines				
e.g. trifluoperazine	low	high	medium	
e.g. chlorpromazine	high	low	medium	
e.g. thioridazine	high	/	medium	
				15–60 mins
Butyrophenome				
e.g. haloperidol	low	high	medium	
				20–120 mins
Others				
e.g. sulpride	low	medium	medium	
e.g. risperidone	/	low	medium	
e.g. pimozide	/	high	medium	
				2–3 hours

Data based on 'BMA: New Guide to Medicine and Drugs'.

Table 4.3: Comparison of different types of neuroleptics

Again there are attempts to discover if one type of neuroleptic is more effective than the others. All groups are better than placebos in reducing the symptoms of the illness and relapse, but the newer drugs (for example, risperidone) are more effective (McGrath and Emerson, 1999).

Anti-anxiety drugs (minor tranquillizers)
In everyday language, these are tranquillizers and are prescribed for anxiety. Their main focus is to reduce the activity in the brain (that is, sedation). But traditionally they have high addiction and overdose ratings (see Table 4.4).

One of the best known groups are barbiturates. Their side effects include concentration problems, lack of co-ordination, slurred speech and withdrawal symptoms, while benzodiazepines (BDZ) include drowsiness, and impaired memory and concentration.

The use of drugs can be controversial because of the strengths and weaknesses (see Table 4.5, page 67), and certainly with children (see RLA 17).

Name	Overdose rating	Depend rating	Onset
Benzodiazepines			
e.g. diazepam	medium	high	0–2 hours
e.g. temazepam	medium	high	15–40 mins
Barbiturates	medium	medium	swift
Beta-blockers			
e.g. oxprenolol	medium	low	1 hour to 2 weeks

Data from 'BMA: New Guide to Medicine and Drugs'.

Table 4.4: Comparison of different types of tranquillizers

Real Life Application 17:

Is it time for my Prozac, mum?

The world of the average toddler is irrational and prone to mood swings when viewed from an adult stance. But does that mean there is something wrong with the average toddler? A USA study found that toddlers were being prescribed psychotropic drugs, and the number had increased between 1991–5.

In Britain, psychiatrists are much more cautious about prescribing psychotropic drugs to pre-school children. Rea Reason, of Manchester University, feels that young children can be difficult without it being labelled as some kind of problem. 'It is more important to understand them than to label them.'

In fact, there is concern that prescribing psychotropic drugs to pre-school children could produce long-term damage to the brain. Animal studies found this when the anti-depressant Prozac was given to baby rats.

The author of the article concludes that 'there is a growing acceptance of drugs as a quick fix for parents who are worried about their children'.

Adapted from 'Is it time for my Prozac, Mum?' by Lucy Atkins, *The Guardian*, 7 March 2000.

Summary

- There is increasing evidence of the use of psychotropic drugs with children, and even pre-school children.

Questions

1 Prozac is a brand name for what type of anti-depressant?

2 Why might Prozac cause long-term brain damage to pre-school children?

3 What is the fastest-growing mental disorder diagnosed for young children in USA?

Electro-Convulsive Therapy (ECT)

Electro-Convulsive Therapy is the concept of inducing a convulsive seizure. It was begun by Ladislas Meduna in the 1930s using insulin and was based on what is now known to be the incorrect

Strengths of drugs	Weaknesses of drugs
1 Drugs do reduce the symptoms of the illness and reduce relapse – e.g. Thronley et al (1997) found that chlorpromazine reduced relapse by nearly half over five years among schizophrenics	1 Side effects – e.g. 50% of takers of Valium (brand name of diazepam) reported drowsiness
2 Gave patients hope of 'cure' rather than being institutionalized for life – e.g. USA mental hospital populations dropped by half in 20 years following introduction of neuroleptics	2 Risks of overdosing and addiction. Neustatter (1991) estimated that 0.25 million people in the UK addicted to minor tranquillizers
3 More humane than earlier methods, like straitjackets	3 Peter Breggin argues that drugs have become a 'chemical straitjacket'; they are prescribed too easily, more often to women, and as a means of controlling patients; and they reduce the symptoms, but do not address the cause of the problem

Table 4.5: Strengths and weaknesses of psychotropic drugs

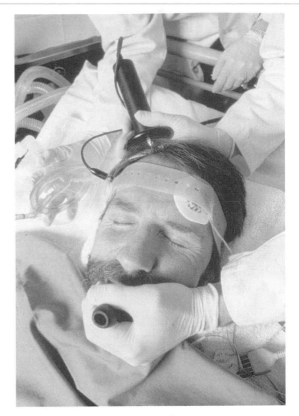

A patient undergoes Electro-Convulsive Therapy.

assumption that epilepsy sufferers are not also psychotic. Cerletti and Bini (1938) then pioneered the use of electricity. Writing in the official Royal College of Psychiatrists ECT Handbook, Freeman (1995) explains the process as 'a seizure which affects the entire brain, including the centres which control thinking, mood, appetite and sleep. Repeated treatments alter chemical messages in the brain and bring them back to normal.' But the effect is not clearly understood.

Modern-day ECT is a controlled technique based on three stages:

1 Preparation: a medical examination of the patient, and no food for six hours beforehand.

2 Administration: an anaesthetic is administered to relax the patient, then a current of electricity is passed through the head for around half a second. This produces unconsciousness and seizure in the patient. The dosage varies between individuals, and there may be a series of treatments (for example, 8–20 treatments at 3 per week).

3 Recovery: the patient is left to recover from the treatment.

Pippard (1992) estimated that 20,000 people annually received ECT in England, one-tenth of whom were given it without their consent under the Mental Health Act. Wise (1997) points out that the figures are biased in certain directions – that is, two to three of all cases are female – while Oxford Health Authority administers 126 treatments per 100,000 people compared to 420 in Cardiff.

ECT is used mainly with severe depressives, particularly in the 1950s before drug treatments were developed, and since the 1970s with drug-resistant depressives. It is also used with other conditions, and this is where the controversy arises.

Peck (1974) entitled his own book *The Miracle of Shock Treatment*, and told how his life was greatly improved by it. But many others tell negative stories. In a MIND report called 'Experiencing Psychiatry' (Rogers *et al*, 1993) 43% reported ECT as helpful or very helpful, while 37% felt it had been unhelpful or very unhelpful. Linda Andre of the Committee for Truth in Psychiatry in the USA reports loss of five years of memories after ECT, and her IQ being reduced by 40 points (see RLA 18, page 68).

Real Life Application 18:

Shock, horror or help?

Jean Taylor, a 65 year old woman, has received ECT more than 50 times in a ten-year period up to 1993. She describes it as the 'most dreadful experience of my life'.

Inducing a seizure by passing electricity through the brain, ECT is performed on around 20,000 people a year in the UK. The charity, MIND, feels that this is too many, and is not being used as the treatment of last resort.

There is a definite division between psychiatrists who support the treatment, and patients who see it as barbaric. Drew Ridley-Siegert, a psychiatrist in Cardiff, sees it as a quicker treatment than drugs. While Jean Taylor threatened to kill herself if she was forced to receive ECT again.

Jacqui Wise, *The Guardian*, 1997.

Strengths of ECT	Weaknesses of ECT
1 Shows improvement for severe depressives	1 Over-used and abused (Clare, 1980); female bias in its use; not used as last resort
2 Necessary for drug-resistant depressives	2 Side effects include memory deficits for 1–6 months after, reading difficulties, painful headaches (Breggin calls it 'fundamentally electrical head injury'); death rate of 3.9 to 9 per 100,000 treatments
3 Quicker and safer than drugs (e.g. no overdosing problems)	3 Not clear how it works; many patients report ECT as punishment for their unhappiness or for being different

Table 4.6: Strengths and weaknesses of ECT

Summary

• ECT is a controversial treatment, and there is a division between psychiatrists who support its use and many patients who do not.

Questions

1 Can ECT be given without the patient's consent?

2 What was the forerunner of ECT?

3 What is the original underlying belief behind the use of ECT?

Jones and Baldwin (1996) highlight the use of ECT with children in the UK (as young as infants). Between 1982 and 1990, 60 children from the UK received ECT compared to between 500 and 3500 per annum in the USA.

The real test of ECT is its success rate – in other words, does it help patients? The answer to this question depends on the study used. For example, Fink (1978), a great supporter of ECT, found a 60%–90% success rate for severe depressives. The measure of success used was not committing suicide in a set period after the treatment. However, Janicek *et al* (1985) reviewed the literature to find that 80% of severely depressed people responded to ECT compared to 64% on TCAs. Other studies only report short-term improvements of less than one month of a depression rating scale.

The strengths and weaknesses of ECT are summarized in Table 4.6.

Psychosurgery

This is by far the most extreme treatment as it involves the destruction of healthy brain tissue. There are several sites in the brain that are targeted. In the past, the method used was to cut the tissue, but currently electrodes are used to burn the tissue or radioactive radium rods.

Psychosurgery is a general name for two different techniques – lobotomy (removal of the brain tissue) and leucotomy (cutting the connections to a particular part of the brain). So, for example, pre-frontal lobotomies and leucotomies focus on tissue that connects the frontal lobes of the cortex to the centre of the brain.

Usually, psychosurgery is reserved for treatment-resistant severe depressives, but it has also been used with those who have chronic anxiety, obsessional disorders and severe epilepsy where other treatments have failed, and those with pathological aggression. The aim is to disconnect the emotions, which are seen as influencing thoughts and causing the problems.

Historically, Egaz Moniz is seen as the inventor of

psychosurgery, and in fact received a Nobel Prize for Medicine (in 1949) for the discovery. He performed around 100 operations between 1935–49. Since the 1930s, there have been around 50,000 operations in the USA alone, while between 1940 and 1950 there were 10,000 operations in Britain. These days, psychosurgery is comparatively rare, with only 26 operations per annum in England and Wales (Cobb, 1993).

Not surprisingly, the use of psychotherapy is very controversial. The supporters argue that everyone is happier afterwards, while Breggin sees it as 'partially killing' the person (see Table 4.7).

Concerning its success rate, there have been a limited number of studies. Cobb (1993) summarized the results as 75% showing improvement, while 25% were unchanged or worse as a result.

Psychodynamic therapy

Psychoanalysis, as used by Sigmund Freud, is seen as the first type of modern therapy. Psychodynamic therapies are those following in the Freudian tradition, but developed by others.

The model of Sigmund Freud's theory of personality and the causes of the problems are discussed in detail in Chapter 2 (see pages 28–30). The main focus, though, is to find the unconscious conflict underlying any psychological problems.

Traditional psychoanalysis

Traditional psychoanalysis as practised by Sigmund

Strengths of psychosurgery	Weaknesses of psychosurgery
1 A last resort in extreme cases: 'A society without psychosurgery available is rendering untreatable some of its most severely ill and desperate people' (Dr. Paul Bridges, quoted in Dobson, 1995)	1 Severe side effects: apathy, insensitivity, memory problems, and 1% risk of death from the operation today; in the past, the risks were greater
2 Calming effect on violent and agitated patients	2 Irreversible: 'Stiff price to pay … if one can't even be sure that … benefits exist' (Gleitman, 1991)
3 Success rate with severe epileptics, who have multiple seizures each day	3 Not clear which regions in the brain to focus upon – e.g. 4 possible places for depression; surgeons have personal preferences

Table 4.7: Strengths and weaknesses of psychosurgery

Freud was based around listening to the patient (analysand) talk, and dream analysis. From this information, Freud built up a picture of what was happening in the unconscious, and then an interpretation of the cause of the problems. As the analysand uses free association (that is, simply talking without interruption or prompting) or word association, the analyst looks for symbolism. For example, a fear of walking down the street may be symbolic of a fear of sexual intercourse. Everything has meaning, but not as it appears to be.

The assumption behind free, or word, association is that all lines of thought lead to what is significant, but the analysand may show resistance (that is, opposed to making conscious what is unconscious).

However, it is not just what is said during analysis. Analysts make their interpretations based on 'forgetting dreams, remaining silent on the couch, trying to convert the treatment into an intellectual discussion of psychoanalytic theory, holding back essential information, being consistently late, treating the analyst as an enemy' (Gay, 1988, p. 299).

Among the non-verbal factors used in analysis is the important concept of transference (and counter-transference). The analyst attempts to be a 'blank screen' on which the analysand portrays childhood feelings. Sadler et al (1970) define transference more technically as 'the displacement of libido from the memory of the original object to the person of the analyst who becomes the new object of the patient's sexual wishes, the patient being unaware of this displacement from the past'. Counter-transference is the analyst's response to this process.

Freud first noticed transference when a female analysand, awaking from hypnosis, put her arms around him and started to kiss him. Freud wanted to know who she was thinking of kissing, rather than taking it at face value.

Modern analysts tend to ask three questions about transference:

1 Who is speaking?
2 To whom is this person speaking?
3 What is the patient talking about and why now?

Again, what is said is not what it appears on the surface.

Freud made a great deal of use of dream analysis and interpretation. He believed dreams to be disguised fulfilment of suppressed wishes. What we remember is the manifest content, while the underlying meaning is known as the latent content.

Psychoanalysis of dreams helps to make sense of latent content, based around three main techniques:

1 Displacement: this is where something appears in manifest content as the substitute for a wish – for example, the queen in a dream means the mother.
2 Condensation: this is where the manifest content can mean many things – for example, the queen can also mean all women.
3 Concrete representation: here an abstract idea is expressed in a concrete way in a dream – for example, the queen could also mean love.

So, for example, a dream about breaking an arm could be a wish to break the marriage vows. Other examples of dream symbols are given in Table 4.8.

Freud also used hypnosis in his early days as a means of discovering what was hidden in the unconscious.

Traditional psychoanalysis can continue indefinitely with (normally) 50-minute sessions four or five times a week. Modern psychoanalysis tends to be short term and has a specific problem-focus (see Table 4.9).

Other psychodynamic techniques

Children are unsuitable for analysis, particulary young children, so Anna Freud (the daughter of Sigmund) developed play therapy. Children are left in a playroom with toys, and their play can be interpreted for the unconscious conflicts. Alternatively, play therapy can be used as a treatment – for example, before an operation, a child plays 'doctors and nurses' to help resolve the anxiety of the operation. This is sometimes known as 'release therapy'. Additionally, the 'mutual storytelling technique' is used

Traditional	Modern
4–5 times per week	1–2 times per week
Use of couch (that is, analyst sits behind analysand)	Face to face
Character reconstruction	Problem resolution
Neutrality of analyst	Active role of analyst
Traditional techniques used	Many techniques; less transference

Table 4.9: Comparison of traditional and modern psychoanalysis

to encourage the child to tell a story based on play, which, again, can be interpreted.

Projective tests are another technique that have their roots in psychodynamics. The best known is the Rorschach Ink-Blot Test (1921). The individual is presented with ten ink-blots and asked to explain what he or she thinks the blots might be. There is no correct answer, simply that what the individual says is interpreted for the underlying meanings. Other projective tests include the Thematic Apperception Test (TAT) (Murray, 1943), and the Menninger Word Association Test (1968).

Since Sigmund Freud was practising analysis, many other psychodynamic theorists have developed their own versions of psychoanalysis. For example, there is Jungian analysis or Kleinian analysis; each with slightly different techniques.

Table 4.10 (see page 71) summarizes the strengths and weaknesses of psychoanalysis generally.

Manifest content	Latent content
king or queen	parents
little animals/vermin	siblings/children
travel/journey	dying
clothes/uniform	nakedness
flying	sexual intercourse
extraction of teeth	castration
water	birth
house	human body
fruit	breasts
rooms, cupboards	womb
receptacles	vagina
number 3	male genitals
sticks, umbrellas, knives, guns, telescopes	penis

Table 4.8: Freudian dream symbols

KEY STUDY 7
Researchers: Eysenck (1952)
Aim: To compare the improvement of neurotic patients following psychoanalysis, eclectic therapy (a combination of techniques) or none at all.
Method: This is a summary of 19 other studies with over 7000 cases. Eysenck's definition of 'cure' was return to work, no further complaint for five years and social readjustment.
Results: 44% of psychoanalysis group showed 'cure', 64% for the eclectic therapy, and 66% for the no

Conclusions: therapy group (spontaneous remission). 'The figures fail to support the hypothesis that psychotherapy (psychoanalysis) facilitates recovery from neurotic disorder' (p. 324). Note that reanalysis of the same data by other researchers has found different results (e.g. Bergin, 1971), and this study has been criticized for its methodology.

Therapies influenced by psychoanalysis

Two types of therapy are influenced by psychoanalysis – transactional analysis and primal therapy.

Transactional Analysis (TA) (Berne, 1968) concentrates on 'life scripts' based around the roles of parent (similar to Sigmund Freud's superego), child (id), and adult (ego).

Primal Therapy (Janov, 1973) concentrates on birth representing the primary trauma in life, from which all other problems stem. The aim is to overcome problems through 'rebirthing'. This therapy is similar to psychoanalysis in accepting that early childhood traumas produce adult neuroses.

Strengths of psychoanalysis	Weaknesses of psychoanalysis
1 Attempts at complete explanation of the human personality, and tries to treat the whole person	1 Traditional psychoanalysis can be lengthy, and there is no clear definition of 'cure' at the end; symptom removal is not necessarily the sign of 'cure'
2 Based on listening to the analysand and what they have to say	2 Researchers have argued that psychoanalysis does not work; Eysenck (1952), in particular, suggests that not only does psychoanalysis not work, but also it is detrimental (see Key Study 7)
3 Aware of hidden conflicts in the unconscious – i.e. the sufferer is often not aware of the underlying cause of their problems	3 The problem of 'recovered memories' or 'false memory syndrome' (see Figure 4.2).

Table 4.10: Strengths and weaknesses of psychoanalysis

This is the controversial issue of clients recalling apparently repressed memories during therapy. Usually it involves traumatic childhood events, like sexual abuse. This can happen in many different types of therapy, and is not exclusive to psychoanalysis.

Even the name used is linked to whether these memories are seen as true or not. Those who support this view call them 'recovered memories', while critics prefer 'false memory syndrome'.

What makes this issue particularly difficult for psychoanalysis is that Sigmund Freud argued that any memories recalled in analysis should be treated as true. This can be called 'narrative truth' – that is, clients believe they occurred and it is affecting their current behaviour. This is different to 'historical truth' – that is, the event actually took place. Some repressed memories that are recalled did happen, while others may not have. The question is how to distinguish between the two.

Tavris and Wade (1995) suggest that scepticism is warranted when:

- clear early memories appear after therapy
- the memories increase in bizarreness with therapy
- the therapist makes diagnosis of sexual abuse early in the sessions
- the therapist uses techniques that alter consciousness, like hypnosis.

In her research on eye-witness testimony, Elizabeth Loftus (1997) has shown that false memories can be planted quite easily. It may not be deliberate by the therapist, but suggestions can become confused with actual memories.

The feeling generally is that sustained abuse would not be completely repressed. Individual events may be repressed, but severe trauma is more likely to produce Post-Traumatic Stress Disorder symptoms (see Chapter 3, pages 38–43), where the event cannot be forgotten.

Prendergrast, quoted in Sutherland, 1997.

Figure 4.2: Problem of 'recovered memories' or 'false memory syndrome'

Behavioural techniques

Behavioural techniques describe a variety of therapeutic methods based on the Behavioural model of abnormality. Usually the distinction is made between Behaviour Therapy, based on the principles of classical conditioning, and Behaviour Modification, using operant conditioning. Full details of the Behavioural model are discussed in Chapter 2 (see pages 26–8).

The main assumption of any behavioural technique is that the maladaptive behaviour has been learnt, and so therapy is a question of learning a more adaptive or more appropriate behaviour.

Behaviour therapy

There are a number of techniques that have been developed on the principles of classical conditioning. This section will outline the three main types of behaviour therapy:

- systematic desensitization
- implosive, or flooding, therapy
- aversion therapy.

Systematic desensitization (SD)

Systematic desensitization is based on the notion of 'reciprocal inhibition' – that is, if a patient responds to an anxiety-provoking stimulus with behaviour that is incompatible with anxiety, the anxiety aroused by the stimulus will be inhibited or weakened. In practice, this means replacing the anxiety or phobic reaction with a non-anxious or non-phobic reaction. This involves the step-by-step reduction of the fear using a hierarchy of acceptable to unacceptable stimuli. Key Study 8 is an early example of SD at work.

The first step in SD is to produce the individual hierarchy with approximately ten to fifteen steps. Then, using the first step – that is, the most acceptable level – the patient is taught to relax or to associate it with a pleasant experience. This takes place over a number of occasions until the patient is

1 See ambulance (most acceptable)
2 See hospital
3 Inside hospital
4 Reading obituary page
5 Pass funeral home
6 Seeing funeral
7 Seeing burial close-up
8 Seeing husband in coffin

Table 4.11: Example of hierarchy based on one used by Wolpe, 1958

entirely happy with that step, then the process begins again for the second step on the hierarchy.

Wolpe (1958) quotes a well-known example of one of his patients who developed a fear of death after the death of her husband (see Table 4.11).

SD is most effective for minor phobias, and for patients who have the ability to relax or with a vivid imagination. It has a clear definition of 'cure', and the patient can chart their progress up the hierarchy. This can be rewarding also.

Implosive, or flooding, therapy

Flooding takes an entirely different approach to SD and induces the patient to come into close proximity to the phobic object without any preliminary coaxing. Implosion encourages the patient to imagine the most frightening encounter for as long as possible. The patient's anxiety is maintained at such a high level that exhaustion occurs and this reduces future anxiety. In another classic example, Wolpe (1960) took a girl afraid of cars, put her in one and drove around for four hours until the fear was removed. The focus of the therapy is when exhaustion occurs because the patient learns to face the phobic object without the fear reaction. This therapy works best for mild phobias again, and with healthy patients.

Aversion therapy

Aversion therapy is used with addictive behaviour to try to teach a dislike for the addictive item. Based on classical conditioning (see Chapter 2, page 27), an unpleasant association is built up with the addicted item. Figure 4.3 (see page 73) gives an example with alcoholics.

Meyer and Cheese (1970) found that 50% of alcoholics who had used this therapy abstained from alcohol for at least one year. But its effectiveness

---

KEY STUDY 8

Researchers: Jones (1924)

Aim:	To remove an extreme fear of rats, rabbits, fur coats, feathers, cotton wool, frogs and fish in a two year old called Peter. This study is often known as 'Little Peter'.
Method:	Using Peter's favourite food, he was introduced slowly to rabbits. In the first session the rabbit was in a cage in the same room. When Peter was happy with this, the next step was to bring the hutch closer. The whole process took 40 sessions and 17 steps.
Results:	At the end of the therapy Peter was happy to stroke the rabbit while eating his favourite food.
Conclusions:	This is an experimental example of systematic desensitization, which is effective for mild fears.

Before conditioning
Unconditioned Stimulus (UCS) ➔ Unconditioned Response
(UCR)
emetic drug   severe vomiting

During conditioning
UCS paired with alcohol   ➔ severe vomiting

After conditioning
Conditioned stimulus (CS)   ➔ Conditioned Response (CR)
alcohol   severe vomiting

Figure 4.3: Example of aversion therapy with alcoholics

depends on the patients being motivated to stop the addictive behaviour. Often relapse is linked to social factors, like the friends still using the addictive substance. It can also be a painful treatment for the patient.

More commonly now, the patient is asked to imagine unpleasant events and associate them with the addictive item. For example, Glover (1985) reports the case of a 56 year old woman who had compulsively shoplifted every day for 14 years. She was given images of vomiting to associate with the shoplifting during 4 therapeutic sessions over 8 weeks. The follow-up 19 months later showed one occasion of shop-lifting only. It is important to have clear imagining and rehearsal of the aversive scenes.

Commentary

Controversially, this therapy has been used with homosexuals to change their sexual preference. Every time they were shown a picture of the same sex, they received a painful electric shock. There is little evidence that it worked.

Behaviour modification

Behaviour modification is a general name for a therapeutic technique based on operant conditioning (see chapter 2, pages 27–8). The main aim is to reward in some way the desired behaviour and punish the undesired behaviour.

Baddeley (1990) lists the steps of any behaviour modification programme as follows:

1 Specify behaviour to change.
2 Set goal to achieve.
3 Set baseline of current maladaptive behaviour.
4 Develop strategy to achieve goal.
5 Plan reinforcement schedule.
6 Treat patient.
7 Monitor behaviour.
8 Change programme if necessary.

Applying this process to the case of Sophie (Colsey and Hatton, 1994), a ten year old girl with severe learning difficulties who is continually injuring herself deliberately, the steps are as follows:

Step 1: throwing herself to floor, biting herself, screaming, hitting herself and others, and throwing objects.
Step 2: stopping these behaviours.
Step 3: an observer measures the behaviours in step 1 to gain an estimate per hour of each behaviour.
Step 4: use of Jaffa cakes as reinforcer for not showing above behaviours.
Step 5: Jaffa cake every time Sophie does not perform those behaviours.
Step 6: over 20 days of programme, undesired behaviour removed.

Behaviour modification has been adapted into the Token Economy System (TES), which is used in hospitals, prisons and schools. This involves the use of plastic tokens as rewards (secondary reinforcers) for desired behaviours, and these tokens can be exchanged for something the individual wants at the end of the week. This system does seem to work, even with chronic schizophrenics in hospital. However, it is not always successful outside the institution – that is, without the tokens.

Table 4.12 summarizes the main strengths and weaknesses of behavioural techniques.

Cognitive behavioural approaches

Cognitive behavioural approaches or cognitive behavioural therapies (CBT) focus on the maladaptive thinking of the sufferer as the cause of the problem. Their aim is thus to change this thinking. Full

Strengths of behavioural techniques	Weaknesses of behavioural techniques
1 Clear goals and steps by which to achieve those goals	1 Discomfort for the patient in many cases
2 Safe compared to physical treatments, with, e.g., no side effects	2 Treats patient in mechanistic way, as product of learning only
3 Based on clear principles of conditioning	3 Behaviour modification often requires thousands of reinforcements to achieve its goals

Table 4.12: Strengths and weaknesses of behavioural techniques

details of the cognitive model underlying CBT are given in Chapter 2 (see pages 30–1).

Sullivan and Rogers (1997) report the case of a 43 year old man, called Michael, who was admitted to hospital after damaging property because he believed people were trying to steal his belongings. His paranoid beliefs focused on four factual unfounded ideas:

1 His stepfather had killed his mother.
2 There was a conspiracy to remove him from his job.
3 He was obsessed with theft from his house.
4 His food had been poisoned on two occasions.

The client was given twelve one-hour sessions, which focused on alternative explanations for his beliefs and challenged him to provide evidence for these paranoid beliefs. Three months later, he still believed there was a conspiracy to remove him from his job, but the strength of the other beliefs had been reduced. The fear of his food being poisoned was almost non-existent.

There are a number of different types of CBT. Two of the main examples – Rational Emotive Therapy and Self-Instructional Training – will be examined in the text that follows.

Rational Emotive Therapy (RET)

This particular type of CBT was developed by Albert Ellis (1962). Ellis identified eleven basic irrational beliefs that underlie problems. These beliefs include 'I must be loved and accepted by absolutely everyone'. For example, Newmark et al (1973) found that 80% of anxious individuals agreed with the statement 'One must be perfectly competent, adequate and achieving to consider oneself worthwhile', compared to 25% of non-anxious individuals. Ellis was particularly interested in the 'should' and 'must' statements that individuals use. Rational Emotive Therapy (RET) challenges the client to prove these statements, and then replaces them with 'realistic' statements.

Ellis (quoted in Gordon, 1987) gives the example of a female client, who was depressed. She was having difficulties finding a boyfriend because she put herself down. She saw herself as a failure all the time, gave up trying and became depressed. Ellis used a variety of techniques to help, as follows:

- Forceful self-statements: the client was encouraged to tell herself: 'It's better to have tried and failed than never tried.'

- Rational emotive imaginary: the client imagined failing, but then only feeling unhappy, not overly critical as she usually did.
- Role playing of different scenarios with the therapist.
- Shame attacking exercises: the client was encouraged to do something 'shameful', then accept herself.
- Cognitive strategies: the client was given information about how to meet men, and relaxation techniques for when she is asked out for a date.
- Behaviour strategies: for example, forcing herself to go out and meet people, and punishing herself for not doing so, rather than just sitting at home.

Haaga and Davidson (1989) reviewed a number of outcome studies on RET. Outcome studies assess the effectiveness of a therapy or treatment. The authors made the following conclusions.

- RET reduces general anxiety, and exam anxiety, based on the self-reports of clients.
- Clients show improvements in social anxiety, but this is inferior to SD.
- RET is inferior to behaviour therapy for treating agoraphobia.
- RET is useful in treating excessive anger, depression and anti-social behaviour.

Self-instructional training

Donald Meichenbaum (1977) believed that problems were due to individuals failing to instruct themselves successfully. Individuals tend to say things to themselves (self-instructions), and these are the basis of emotions and behaviour.

SIT programmes tend to have four distinct steps, whatever the problem being addressed.

1 Individuals state to themselves the requirements of the task. The task here means the required behaviour.
2 Individuals then instruct themselves to perform the task slowly and to think before acting.
3 Individuals develop cognitive strategies for dealing with the task, and imagine themselves carrying them out.
4 Self-reward strategies are used if the above steps are successful. If not, self-statements are developed about how to cope with failure and overcome the problems.

Meichenbaum and Goodman (1971) achieved success with a SIT programme to limit the impulsive behaviour of hyperactive children. Here is an example of how the programme may work:

Step 1: the task is to sit at the desk for fifteen minutes and carry out the schoolwork. The child clearly states the task for himself (or herself).

Step 2: the child talks to himself/herself as he/she performs the task.

Step 3: the child uses strategies to stop his/her impulsive behaviour, like counting to five before he/she acts. The child practises the strategies.

Step 4: rewards are gained for achieving the task, and using the cognitive strategies.

SIT programmes are commonly used as the basis of stress management, and anxiety reduction techniques. Meichenbaum (1972) found SIT to be more effective than SD in helping anxious students reduce their worries about work.

Table 4.13 summarizes the strengths and weaknesses of CBT.

Humanistic therapy

Therapies under this heading are different to the other approaches outlined so far in this chapter. The difference is twofold: the aim is to understand the world from the client's viewpoint, and there are no real techniques for changes used. It is assumed that by understanding the clients' view of the world, and supporting them with empathy and unconditional positive regard, they will be able to help themselves. Full details of the humanistic model are contained in Chapter 2 (see pages 31–3).

Client-centred therapy (CCT)

Based on the ideas of Carl Rogers (1951), who is seen as the founder of the humanistic movement in psychology, CCT focuses on the clients and their views of the world. Problems are caused by a lack of congruence between experience and the self-concept – for example, a 'successful' individual might feel that he or she is not 'successful'.

The aim of the therapy is to understand why the individual feels this way, and to help that individual to help him or herself. The role of the therapist is to accept clients and support them. What is very different here is that therapists may self-disclose about themselves and their own experiences. Traditionally psychotherapy has discouraged this behaviour by the therapist. It is the clients themselves who have the capacity to understand and solve their problems.

Measuring the effectiveness of this type of therapy is difficult. But Butler and Haigh (1954), in one of the few studies, used the gap between the current self-image and the ideal self. The larger the gap is seen as a sign of incongruence. After six weeks of CCT, this gap had been reduced, compared to a control group not in therapy.

Encounter groups

Also known as 'T groups' or 'sensitivity training groups', these are groups that aim to improve the self-esteem of members by empathy and unconditional positive regard by the whole group. Only positive comments will be made about each member of the group. For example, one by one the members say what they like about a specific group member.

Personal construct therapy (PCT)

George Kelly (1955) focused on the constructs that the individual uses to understand the world. A construct is a way of seeing and predicting the world, usually based on bipolar dimensions, like trustworthy-untrustworthy. The individual may have four or five core constructs, as well as subordinate ones. These are the basis of the individual's whole view of the world.

Problems are caused if the constructs are consistently invalidated – for example, anxiety is where the constructs are inadequate or inappropriate to events.

The aim of PCT is to change the constructs to make better sense, and more accurately predict the world. The therapist and client work together, usually with the Repertory Grid Technique (RGT) (for an example of one of these, see Figure 4.4, page 76). This technique makes clear the constructs the client is using to view the world. For example, the client

Strengths of CBT	Weaknesses of CBT
1 Takes account of individuals' thinking processes, and how they view the world	1 Only possible with clients who can reflect on their own thoughts
2 Clear goal for the treatment - to change the maladaptive thinking	2 Ignores hidden reasons for problems, like unconscious thoughts
3 Is effective for less serious problems	3 Changing thinking patterns may not be enough to remove more severe problems

Table 4.13: Strengths and weaknesses of CBT

Andy's current view of a sample of his work colleagues:

Similarity pole (x)	Dave	John	Cathy	Alan	Difference pole (*)
lacks awareness	x	x	*	x	has awareness
not to be trusted	x	*	*	*	can be trusted
committed	*	*	x	*	just a job
effective	*	*	x	x	never finishes what he/she starts
creative	x	x	*	*	unimaginative

Figure 4.4: Example of repertory grid

thinks of characteristics by which two elements (for example, friends) are similar and a third is different. This process continues with a number of elements to give the pattern of bipolar constructs.

A variation on PCT is known as 'fixed role therapy'. The client creates a 'role sketch' of who they would like to be. The client is encouraged to act out the role and develop new personal constructs. In time, it is hoped, this will lead to the changing of the original constructs.

Table 4.14 summarizes the strengths and weaknesses of humanistic therapy.

Evaluating therapies and treatments

In evaluating therapies and treatments, there are two questions that are asked:

1 Does it work compared to no treatment?
2 Which therapy or treatment is best?

Concerning the first question, there are many stud-ies comparing treatments and therapies with placebo and no therapy groups. The general conclusion is that any therapy is better than none.

As for the second question, no single therapy or treatment comes out as the best in all situations. It is easier to summarize the characteristics of successful therapists as giving their clients a high level of unconditional positive regard, providing a warm relationship between the them and their clients, and using some kind of technique to encourage change (Frank, 1974).

On the patient's side, intelligent and educated individuals whose problems are not too great and who have a positive attitude towards therapy will benefit most.

Outcome studies tend to face a number of problems, as outlined below.

- Individuals can improve just because they expect to improve, not because of the therapy.
- Paying attention to individuals can be enough for them to improve ('Hawthorne effect').
- Some individuals can improve without any help ('spontaneous remission').
- Different therapies and treatments have different definitions of 'cure'.

Thus the original questions are not applicable. Ryle (1975) argues that we should ask: 'What kinds of patients can change in what kinds of ways through what kinds of therapy?'

Ethics and treatment

In the same way that psychologists have to be aware of the ethics of experimenting with participants, there are ethical issues for therapists. The *Guidelines for Professional Practice of Clinical Psychology* (1983) outlines five ethical principles.

1 Maintaining professional competence.
2 Not giving a false impression of competence.

Strengths of humanistic therapy	Weaknesses of humanistic therapy
1 Focuses on understanding how clients view the world rather than imposing views upon them	1 Some clients need actual help and techniques for change, rather than just empathy and unconditional positive regard
2 Treats the whole person rather than just a problem	2 Too much unconditional positive regard may give the client unrealistic expectations of the future
3 Encourages clients to solve their own problems rather than to depend on a therapist.	3 Only really effective for clients with low self-esteem and a general unhappiness with life, but not more serious problems

Table 4.14: Strengths and weaknesses of humanistic therapy

3 Safeguards for the work of trainees.

4 Obtaining valid consent from clients for treatment.

5 Maintaining the client's privacy and confidentiality.

In practice, these guidelines are not as straightforward as they appear – for example, under the Prevention of Terrorism Act (1989) information must be disclosed to prevent terrorism; the same applies to child abuse under the Children Act (1989).

There are cases of the abuse of power by therapists in the relationships that develop with clients. Garrett (1994) found that up to 7% of USA psychiatrists admitted 'sexual contact' with their clients, while the figure was nearer 4% for the UK (Garrett and Davis, 1994).

Other ethical issues in treatment include:

- how to gain informed consent from clients who are very ill and, if psychotic, who have lost touch with reality

- balancing the physical discomfort of the treatment with its effectiveness – for example, all drugs have side effects

- how much control and how directive the therapist should be with the client

- the fact that therapists cannot be neutral, so how much of their own values are they imposing on their clients? This can show itself in differences between the therapist and the client over gender, 'race', and sexuality (Gross, 1998).

Essay questions

1 Compare and contrast two types of therapy.

2 Compare and contrast two techniques for dealing with depression.

3 Compare and contrast somatic and behavioural therapies.

A Advice on answering essay questions

Chapter 1

All three questions are looking for similar material, though the emphasis will be different. The main material is a comparison of the different definitions of abnormality, including norms, mental health and mental illness. The better answers will include examples from different cultures and sub-cultures, and will also evaluate each definition. Each definition has both strengths and weaknesses.

Chapter 2

1 This essay will be based around the three assumptions of the medical model. The essay needs to give details of each one and, ideally, evaluate each assumption. The best answers may include reference to other models.

2 and 3 Both these questions require a comparison of two approaches. In each case, it is necessary first to outline the main assumptions of each model, and then to show the strengths and weaknesses of each one. Better answers will directly compare and contrast throughout the answer rather than simply listing one approach followed by the other.

Chapter 3

1 It is important to outline the symptoms of phobias initially. The question requires more than one explanation. In an exam, time may limit the explanations used to two or three only. The explanations chosen will include the underlying model and cause of the phobic behaviour. The better answers will compare and contrast as they go along.

2 The answer should include the symptoms of anorexia and bulimia, then details of the main explanations. The better answers will show how there are multiple causes.

3 This is a nature versus nurture question on schizophrenia. It is necessary to outline both sides of the argument. The better answers will see a combination of the two sides – for example, vulnerability model.

Chapter 4

All three questions are basically the same, and typical of exam questions. It is important to outline the models on which the chosen techniques are based. In describing the actual techniques, the better answers will show how they are trying to achieve their aims. Evaluation should include whether the techniques are effective, and how they define 'cure'.

A Advice on answering short answer questions

Chapter 1

RLA 1

1 Yes, if that is the social norm.

2 Not by criteria of schizophrenia.

3 It depends on the definition applied.

RLA 2

1 These are symptoms of the eating disorder known as bulimia. In the long term this cycle of starving, bingeing and vomiting is physically unhealthy.

2 In this society, 'shopping therapy' has become a popular activity – that is, a belief that buying things will make you happy, whether you can afford them or not. Statistically, many people have credit card debts.

3 Bob is showing the signs of alcohol addiction. However, this type of behaviour is partly acceptable as a way that men can express their unhappiness in this society, while women may use 'shopping therapy'. The consumption of large amounts of alcohol by men is a statistically normal activity.

4 Sexual intercourse before the age of sixteen is illegal in Britain.

5 Technically this is defined as 'transvestic fetishism' in DSM IV, but usually it is associated with sexual arousal from wearing women's clothes by heterosexual men.

6 The belief that collecting newspapers is his calling may be delusional, or he may be eccentric.

RLA 3

1 Not normal.

2 Social norms; statistical norms, in particular.

3 No. Other societies have no problem with not wearing clothes.

RLA 4

1 Number of psychiatric admissions; daily dosage of particular drugs.

2 Social constructions.

3 Greater choice in life decisions; benefits of education like reading; education as empowerment/liberation.

RLA 5

1 Treatment – because it attempts to change the body in some way.

2 Because of 'shellshock', experienced by many soldiers.

3 Only females experience it.

RLA 6

1 He has delusions based on skin colour, name or heir to throne.

2 'Sectioned'.

3 'Removal to place of safety'.

Chapter 2

RLA 7

Case 1: paranoid schizophrenia – three key symptoms shown are hearing voices; thought disorders (for example, thought being transmitted); and primary delusions (for example, belief that thoughts affect the world).

Case 2: obsessive-compulsive disorder – obsessive thoughts of dirtiness and ritualistic compulsion to wash hands.

Case 3: normal personality – anxiety experienced is common to others in a similar position.

RLA 8

1 The most reported stigma is 'dangerous to oth-

ers'. But people suffering from mental illness are rarely violent.

2 Talking to self – for example, in prayer or thinking out loud.

3 UFO sightings or abductions.

RLA 9

1 Category 2: mental illnesses that resemble Western categories (major depressive disorder).

2 Category 5: cultural interpretations of behaviour that are not acceptable in Western psychiatry.

3 Category 1: local mental illnesses that do not have Western categories.

RLA 10

1 Anxiety.

2 Conversion disorder – physical symptoms having anxiety as cause.

3 Breathlessness.

RLA 11

1 Yes; because it is seen as part of science, which is often antagonistic to spiritual matters.

2 Yes; family therapy or group psychotherapy.

3 In Asia traditionally self-awareness and insight are important, while this is not so in Africa.

Chapter 3

RLA 12

1 The phobia is learnt through classical conditioning – for example, the classical conditioning of the phobic item with an unpleasant experience, like the chocolate bar and the dead body.

2 Social phobia.

3 Women are more likely to suffer from agoraphobia and men from social phobia.

RLA 13

1 Emotional.

2 Learned helplessness.

3 Dispositional attribution; this blames the individual for his/her own problems.

RLA 14

1 A general term to cover attempted and successful suicides.

2 Social learning theory and the work of Albert Bandura on observational learning.

3 Because the second and third weeks after the programme saw a drop in such cases compared to the usual average. Thus the effect of the programmes was greatest in the week following its transmission.

RLA 15

1 The images of unrealistic and unobtainable physically attractive male bodies as the ideal – that is, the pressure to look like that in order to get a partner.

2 Binge and then purge.

3 White, teenage, female, middle-class.

RLA 16

1 Behaviourist – that is, reinforcement and punishment.

2 Because problems with food are usually a sign of other emotional problems.

3 Refeeding, using oral, naso-gastric or intravenous delivery.

Chapter 4

RLA 17

1 Selective serotonin reuptake inhibitors (SSRI).

2 Because their brains are still growing and the strength of the dosage is based on adult neuro-chemistry.

3 Attention Deficit Hyperactivity Disorder (ADHD).

RLA 18

1 Yes, under the Mental Health Act 1983, if the patient is 'sectioned'.

2 Insulin-induced seizures.

3 That epileptics are not also psychotic. This has been proved to be an incorrect assumption.

B) Selected references

Abercrombie, N et al (1988). *Contemporary British Society*. Cambridge: Polity Press.

Atkinson, RL, Atkinson, RC, Smith, EE & Bem, DJ (1990). *Introduction to Psychology* (tenth edition). New York: Harcourt Brace Jovanovich.

Banyard, P (2000). 'Why war?' *Psychology Review*, February, pp. 16-19.

Bennett-Levy, J & Marteau, J (1984). 'Fear of animals: what is prepared?' *British Journal of Psychology*, 75, pp. 37-42.

Bhui, K et al (1998). 'Afro-Caribbean men remanded in Brixton prison.' *British Journal of Psychiatry*, 172, pp. 337-44.

Brosnan, MJ & Davidson, MJ (1994). 'Computerphobia – is it a particular female phenomenon?' *Psychologist*, February, pp. 73-8.

Button, EJ, Sonuga-Barke, EJS, Davies, J & Thompson, M (1996). 'A prospective study of self-esteem in the prediction of eating problems in adolescent schoolgirls: questionnaire findings.' *British Journal of Clinical Psychology*, 35, pp. 193-203.

Chadwick, PK (1997). *Schizophrenia: The Positive Perspective*. London: Routledge, p. 3.

Cheasty, M, Clare, AW & Collins, C (1998). 'Relationship between sexual abuse in childhood and adult depression: case control study.' *British Medical Journal*, 17 January, pp. 198-201.

Chief Medical Officer (1995). *On the State of Public Health*. London: HMSO.

Cialdini, RB (1996). 'Social Norms'. In Kuper, A & Kuper, J (eds) *Social Sciences Encyclopaedia* (second edition). London: Routledge.

Clamp, A (1999). 'Anxiety and eating disorders.' *Psychology Review*, September, pp. 20-3.

Cobb, A (1993). *Safe and Effective?* London: MIND.

Cobb, A (1996). 'Making sense of the process and effects of ECT.' *Nursing Times*, 6 March, pp. 32-3.

Cochrane, R (1995). 'Women and depression.' *Psychology Review*, September, pp. 20-4.

Coppock, V & Hopton, J (2000). *Critical Perspectives on Mental Health*. London: Routledge.

Davies, S et al (1996). 'Ethnic differences in risk of compulsory psychiatric admission among representative cases of psychosis.' *London British Medical Journal*, 312, pp. 533-7.

Davison, GC & Neale, JM (1994). *Abnormal Psychology* (sixth edition). Chichester: John Wiley.

Dyer, C (1996). 'Spotting a killer.' *The Guardian*, part 2, 30 July, p.5.

Fernando, S (1992). *Mental Health, Race and Culture*. Basingstoke: Macmillan.

Focus Dossier (1995). 'Soldiering on in the media age.' *Focus*, April, pp. 32-6.

Gay, P (1988). *Freud: A Life for Our Times*. London: JM Dent.

Gleitman, H (1991). *Psychology* (third edition). New York: WW Norton.

Gordon, J (1987). 'RET:II Basic clinical theory and practice.' *Counselling*, November, pp. 18-26.

Gorenstein, EE (1984). 'Debating mental illness.' *American Psychologist*, 39, 1, pp. 50-6.

Gross, R (1998). 'Neutral Therapy?' *Psychology Review*, April, 16-18.

Hagan, J (1984). *The Disreputable Pleasures*. Toronto: McGraw-Hill.

Hawton, K et al (1999). 'Effect of a drug overdose in a TV drama on presentation to hospital for self poisoning.' *British Medical Journal*, 10 April, pp. 972-7.

Herman, D and Green, J (1991). *Madness: A Study Guide*. London: BBC Education.

Hofberg, K & Brockington, I (2000). 'Tokophobia.' *British Journal of Psychiatry*, 176, pp. 83-5.

Hotopf, M, Hardy, R and Lewis, G (1997). 'Discontinuation rates are same for SSRIs and newer TCA and HCA.' *Evidence-Based Medicine*, September/October, p. 149.

Humphreys, P (1997). '(Ab)normality.' *Psychology Review*, 3, 4, pp. 10-15.

Humphreys, P (1999). 'Culture Bound Syndromes.' *Psychology Review*, 5, 2, pp. 14-18.

Hurd, G *et al* (1986). *Human Societies* (revised). London: Routledge.

Illman, J (1997). 'Studies in melancholy.' *The Guardian*, part 2, 14 October, pp. 4-5.

Jahoda, M (1958). *Current Concepts of Positive Mental Health*. New York: Basic Books.

Jamison, KR (1995). 'Manic-depressive illness and creativity.' *Scientific American*, February, pp. 46-51.

Johnstone, L (1993). 'Psychiatry: are we allowed to disagree?' *Clinical Psychology Forum*, June, pp. 30-2.

Jones, Y & Baldwin, S (1996). 'ECT, infants, children and adolescents.' *Behavioural and Cognitive Psychotherapy*, 24, 4, pp. 291-306.

Joseph, S *et al* (1997). 'Attitudes towards emotional expression and post-traumatic stress in survivors of "Herald of Free Enterprise" disaster.' *British Journal of Clinical Psychology*, 36, pp. 133-8.

Kaplan, HI & Sadock, BJ (1998). *Synopsis of Psychiatry* (eighth edition). Baltimore: Williams and Wilkins.

Kiev, A (1972). *Transcultural Psychiatry*. Harmondsworth: Penguin.

King, DW *et al* (1999). 'Post-traumatic stress disorder in a national sample of female and male Vietnam veterans.' *Journal of Abnormal Psychology*, 108, 1, pp. 164-70.

Lang, G (1997). 'In search of perfection.' *Psychology Review*, November, pp. 24-5.

Leff, J (1992). 'Over the edge.' *New Scientist*, 4 January, pp. 30-3.

Lehane, M (1996). 'What the papers say.' *Nursing Standard*, 3 April, pp. 22-3.

Link, BG & Phelan, JC (1999). 'Labelling and stigma.' In Aneshensel, CS and Phelan, JC (eds) *Handbook of the Sociology of Mental Health*. New York: Kluwer Academic/Plenum Publishers, 1972.

Lloyd, A (1991). 'Altered states.' *The Guardian*, 25 June, p. 36.

Loftus, E (1997). 'Creating false memory.' *Scientific American*, September, pp. 51-5.

Lovanger, AW (1984). 'Sex differences in age at onset of schizophrenia.' *Archives of General Psychiatry*, 41, pp, 157-61.

McCreadie, RG *et al* (1997). 'Nithsdale, Nunhead and Norwood.' *British Journal of Psychiatry*, 170, pp. 31-6.

Maciejowski, PK, Prigerson, HG & Mazure, CM (2000). 'Self-efficacy as mediator between stressful life events and depressive symptoms.' *British Journal of Psychiatry*, 176, pp. 373-8.

Malkin, AR *et al* (1999). 'Women and weight.' *Sex Roles*, 40, 7-8, pp. 647-56.

Mukai, T (1996). 'Predictors for relapse and chronicity in eating disorders: a review of follow-up studies.' *Japanese Psychological Review*, 38, 2, pp. 97-105.

Nandi, DN *et al* (2000). 'Psychiatric morbidity of a rural Indian community.' *British Journal of Psychiatry*, 176, pp. 351-6.

O'Brien, LS (1998). *Traumatic Events and Mental Health*. Cambridge: Cambridge University Press.

Office for National Statistics (2000). *Social Trends 30*. London: ONS.

Orbach, S (1993). *Hunger Strike* (second edition). Harmondsworth: Penguin.

Pathare, SR & Paton, C (1997). 'Psychotropic drug treatment.' *British Medical Journal*, 13 September, pp. 661-4.

Paton, D (1992). 'Disaster research: Scottish dimension.' *Psychologist*, December, pp. 535-8.

Pendick, D (2000). 'Caught napping.' *New Scientist*, 26 February, pp. 42-5.

Petkova, B (1995). 'New views on the self.' *Psychology Review*, 2, 1, pp. 16-19.

Petkova, B (1997). 'Understanding eating disorders.' *Psychology Review*, September, pp. 2-7.

Poirer & Boyer (1999). 'Venlafaxine and paroxetine in treatment-resistant depression.' *British Journal of Psychiatry*, 175, pp. 12-16.

Prentice, P (1995). 'Rational Emotive Therapy.' *Psychology Review*, November, pp. 28-31.

Prentice, P (1996). 'Meichenbaum's Self-Instructional Training.' *Psychology Review*, April, pp. 12-14.

Prins, H (1990). *Bizarre Behaviours*. London: Routledge.

Pye, J (1996). 'Eating disorders – recognition of symptoms.' *Special Needs Information Press*, January, pp. 1-3.

Robins, LN *et al* (1984). 'Lifetime prevalence of specific psychiatric disorders in 3 sites.' *Archives of General Psychiatry*, 41, pp. 949-58.

Rosenhan, DL & Seligman, MEP (1995). *Abnormal Psychology* (third edition). London: Norton.

Sadgrove, J (1996). 'Calling all party poopers.' *The Guardian*, part 2, 10 December, pp. 4-5.

Saul, H (1993). 'Phobias: is there a way out?' *New Scientist*, 18 December, pp. 23-5.

Sayal, A (1990). 'Black women and mental health.' *Psychologist*, January, pp. 24-7.

Sayce, L (1999). 'High time for justice.' *Nursing Times*, 3 March, pp. 64-6.

Sayce, L (2000). *Psychiatric Patient to Citizen*. Basingstoke: Macmillan.

Seymour-Smith, C (1986). *Macmillan Dictionary of Anthroplogy*. London: Palgrave.

Shaw, CM *et al* (1999). 'Prevalence of anxiety and depressive illness and help-seeking behaviour among Afro-Caribbean and white Europeans.' *British Medical Journal*, 30 January, pp. 302-6.

Spigset, O & Martensson, B (1999). 'Drug treatment of depression.' *British Medical Journal*, 1 May, pp. 1188-91.

Spitzer, BL *et al* (1999). 'Gender differences in population vs media body sizes.' *Sex Roles*, 40, 7-8, pp. 545-65.

Staff Writer (1998). 'Spirit of the age.' *The Economist*, 19 December, pp. 123-9.

Stallard, P, Velleman, R & Baldwin, S (1998). 'Prospective study of post-traumatic stress disorder in children involved in road traffic accidents.' *British Medical Journal*, 12 December, pp. 1619-23.

Stevens, R (1996). 'The reflexive self: an experiential perspective.' In Stevens, R (ed.) *Understanding the Self*. London: Sage.

Stirling, J, Hellewell, J & Moore, A (1999). 'Schizophrenia: the causes may be out there.' *Psychology Review*, November, pp. 2-5.

Stix, G (1996). 'Listening to culture.' *Scientific American*, January, pp. 8-9.

Sullivan, J & Rogers, P (1997). 'Cognitive behavioural nursing therapy in paranoid psychosis.' *Nursing Times*, 8 January, pp. 28-30.

Takei, N *et al* (1998). 'First episodes of psychosis in Afro-Caribbean and white people.' *British Journal of Psychiatry*, 172, pp. 337-44.

Thornley, B, Adams, CE & Awad, G (1997). 'Chlorpromazine vs placebo for those who are schizophrenic.' *Evidence-Based Medicine*, November/December, p. 1998.

Veysey, G *et al* (1999). 'Anti-freeze poisonings give more insight into copycat behaviour.' *British Medical Journal*, 23 October, p. 1131.

Weeks, D & James, J (1995). *Eccentrics*. London: Weidenfield & Nicolson.

Wessely, S (1997). 'Epidemiology of crime, violence and schizophrenia.' *British Journal of Psychiatry* supplement, 32, pp. 8-11.

Wetherell, M & Maybin, J (1996). 'The distributed self: a social constructionist perspective.' In Stevens, R (ed.) *Understanding the Self*. London: Sage.

Weiss, D (1989). '100% American.' *Daily Telegraph*, 12 August, p. 13.

Williams, RM (1968). 'Norms' in Sills, DL (ed.) *International Encyclopaedia of Social Sciences*. New York: Macmillan Co. & The Free Press.

Williamson, I (1999). 'Why are gay men a high risk group for eating disorders?' *European Eating Disorders Review*, 7, 1, pp. 1-4.

Williamson, I & Hartley, P (1998). 'British research into increased vulnerability of young gay men to eating disorders and body dissatisfaction.' *European Eating Disorders Review*, 6, 3, pp. 160-70.

Wood, D (1993). *The Power of Words: Uses and Abuses of Talking Treatment*. London: MIND.

Yarney, G (1999). 'Young less tolerant of mentally ill than old.' *British Journal of Psychiatry*, 174, p. 1092.

RADIO

All in the Mind (1991). 'What is mental health?' BBC Radio 4.

All in the Mind (1992). 'Fear.' BBC Radio 4.

All in the Mind (1995). 'How the media portrays mental illness.' BBC Radio 4.

All in the Mind (1995). Peter Campbell; BBC Radio 4.

All in the Mind (1999). 'Increase in male suicide.' BBC Radio 4.

Medicine now (1994). 'Are British psychiatrists racist?' BBC Radio 4.

Science Now (1995). Jonathan Flint; BBC Radio 4.

Science Now (1995). Mark Williams; 'Suicide and memory triggers.' BBC Radio 4.

States of Mind (1996). 'Don't fence me in.' BBC Radio 4.

You and Yours (1993). 'Dentist phobia.' BBC Radio 4.

TELEVISION

Depression (1996). 'Moving On.' RCN Nursing Update.

Discover Magazine (1997). 'Fear.' Discovery Channel.

Discovering Psychology (1987). 'Psychopathology.' The Learning Channel.

Enemy Within (1995). 'Agoraphobia: Stephanie Cole.' BBC.

Enemy Within (1995). 'Eating Disorders: Michaela Strachen.' BBC.

Enemy Within (1995). 'Post-traumatic Stress Disorder: Adam Faith.' BBC.

Horizon (1999). 'Living on Air.' BBC.

In Two Minds (1991). 'Madness.' BBC.

Irrational Behaviour, source unknown.

Living Hell (1999). BBC .

Madness (1991). 'To Define True Madness.' BBC.

Minders (1995). 'Whose Mind Is It Anyway?' BBC.

Shellshock (1998). Channel 4.

World in Action (1994). 'Fatal Presciption.' Granada.

Index